THE WILLIAM J. COOPER FOUNDATION

LECTURES 1937

SWARTHMORE COLLEGE

# THEORY AND PRACTICE
## IN
# INTERNATIONAL RELATIONS

# THEORY AND PRACTICE
## IN
# INTERNATIONAL
# RELATIONS

By

Salvador de Madariaga

UNIVERSITY OF PENNSYLVANIA PRESS

Philadelphia

1937

# CONTENTS

# I

# THEORY AND PRACTICE
# IN INTERNATIONAL
# RELATIONS

THE series of five lectures which have been entrusted to my care by the Cooper Foundation and Swarthmore College bear on the question of the theory and practice of international relations. In the rapid and all too flattering sketch which he has made before you of my career, President Aydelotte has reminded you of the practical part which I have had to take in international relations in the last fifteen years or so, first as a member of the League Secretariat, especially entrusted with the question of disarmament, then as Spanish delegate to the League Council and Assembly. Yet it is not as a man of action that I come before you. For we are here fundamentally in a house of learning; we are here, therefore, exclusively to serve truth.

On the walls of one of the universities that I have recently visited in this country there is a proud motto carved into the stone—"Truth will make you free." The trouble is that even for those of us who do not wash our hands of it, like the Roman Governor of Palestine, truth is a very difficult thing to define. But if not actual and complete truth, the real and sincere attempt at getting at truth is the norm, is the law of an institution such as this. Now, truth for the man of affairs, truth for the man who has to deal with international or with national affairs in a public forum is not exactly the same as truth for the man who is bent on a process of investigation. For us—and I crave permission to put myself now along with you as among those who are in search of truth—for us truth is an aim, it is that which we are looking for, that which we want to get at, and for truth we are ready to sacrifice many a thing, many a convenience, many an affection, sometimes even many a courtesy. But the politician, the statesman, the man of affairs, the public man who is handling quite an entirely different material, called action, uses truth in a quite different way. Not that he deliberately omits it, falsifies it, or administers it niggardly; but, more often than not, he may be tempted to use it as an instrument rather than as an aim. And let us be happy when he is not tempted to use it as a projectile!

I shall endeavor, then, with you, to work my way toward truth and in the sincere desire of putting before you the experiences of a man who was temporarily taken away from his real vocation, that of a man of thought, into the field of action. In this way I may, perhaps, have to put before you now and then—I do not know, perhaps not, but I may have to put before you—ideas, suggestions, points of view that may be unfamiliar or even unpleasant to you. If it were so, I should like you to be good enough to take it as the painful obligation of a man who puts his desire for truthful expression before everything.

### INTERNATIONAL RELATIONS A FORM OF POLITICS

We are then going to speak about international relations, and obviously international relations are a form of politics. They are one of the forms that politics take. It might then be good if we attempted to reach our own synthetic view of politics themselves, and surely they can be defined in many ways; but for my purpose I should like to be allowed to define them as *the mechanics of collective forces*. President Aydelotte told you a minute ago that I started my work as an engineer. I started my work as a mathematician and a student of rational mechanics, which is the name of the science of physical forces from the theoretical point of view. Well then, politics, I sometimes fancy, might be defined as irrational mechanics, that is to say the mechanics of collective forces.

You may want to know what I understand by collective forces. I call *collective forces all manifestations of life endowed with power to influence collective events*. For example, courage, intelligence, and power of persuasion in a leader, or in a man placed in a strategic position within the community, is a collective force. Cohesion in a group of persons also placed by life in a strategic position—for instance, the workers who control electric power in a community—is also a collective force. But if this be the case, we quickly come to the conclusion that in life, in collective life, there are very few forces that are not collective forces, so that forces which might seem to be physical are—I dread to use the word "moral" forces, because most moral forces are immoral, but if you will take my point, this reservation having been made, then I will make bold to say—are in reality moral forces.

Physical forces, even in such forms as look most like tyranny, are not really material forces, they are moral forces, for physical force never goes beyond that of one single individual, and even in him it has behind it the moral force of the courage necessary to administer the physical force possessed by that individual. But on the day on which two men come together and unite their physical force, that union can only arise out of an agreement as to the aims to which this physical force of those two men is to be applied; therefore, the physical force of two men is already a moral force.

*The physical force of two soldiers is already an institution.* It is discipline or at least an agreement between those two soldiers. It may be due to bilateral agreement between them or to the effect of discipline on both. In any case, it is already a moral force.

It follows that the State is based entirely on moral forces and therefore, the State (with a capital S) depends—if you will allow me this indulgence in verbal play—on the state (with a small s) of the moral forces of the community in question. Hence in many ways that expression, "a State," may be perhaps more profound than it might at first appear. The State (with a capital S) depends on the state (with a small s) of the moral forces of the individuals, entities, that compose it. This is a most important observation for national life. It is far more important still for international life, and much gnashing of teeth, and much disappointment, might have been avoided if people had realized that it is impossible to expect of a world community which is groping toward its State (with a capital S), that it should go further and rise higher and become more efficient than the state (with a small s) of the moral forces which compose it allows. We cannot go beyond the general state or level of the moral forces that guide us! Just as the education of a nation cannot rise higher than the average level of the education of its educationalists, and just as the justice of a State cannot rise higher than the general level of the spirit of justice of its judges, just so it is impossible that the world community should rise higher, i. e., that the degree of international and public morality should rise higher than the morality of the entities and individuals that compose it, or, in other words, of the morality of the nations and individuals that compose it.

Now the problems of collective life in politics resemble

very closely the problems of mechanics, in that what is wanted for solving them, for judging them, for foreseeing what is going to happen, is an adequate estimate of the forces that are present, an adequate estimate of the direction of those forces, of their sense and of their intensity. And we estimate the political acumen of men at their capacity for estimating these forces, their direction, their intensity, and their sense. If we are observing events and we forget one of the important forces present, we shall certainly be very far wrong in our estimate of the results; and it happens constantly to all of us that we are surprised at seeing a situation come out of its knot in a direction that we did not expect, because when we were trying to estimate the situation we forgot one or more of the important forces that went to the composition of it. Hence the training of rational mechanics should be excellent for this study of irrational mechanics which is politics, in that it trains the mind not to forget any of the elements that act on the situation.

### SOLIDARITY—SUBJECTIVE AND OBJECTIVE

The milieu in which we are going to study these principles is the world community. And the world community resembles every other community in that it may be defined by the solidarity which binds together all its members. There are two kinds of solidarity of an entirely different description, and the distinction between the two is essential for the estimate of international affairs—indeed, of any affairs of any community.

*Solidarity may be defined as the interdependence between parts of a whole, without which the whole does not exist.* Here again you will allow me to make a material comparison. While today physicists and chemists and mathematical physio-chemists are more or less lost in their description of the intimacy of matter, in the days in which these things were less complicated we were all told that matter could be explained by the balance, the state of equilibrium, between a force that kept together the atoms and the force that tended to make them disperse, the cohesive and the dispersive forces. Now in a community we may observe the tendency of every individual to be left alone and to do what he pleases, a tendency which acts as a dispersive force; and, at the same time, something else, rather elusive and difficult to define, which acts as a cohesive force. If this cohesive force does not exist there is no community. But if it exists in a sufficient degree to counterbalance the dispersive tendency of the individual, then we are in the presence of a community.

This cohesive force is what I understand as solidarity. I call *objective solidarity* that which obtains in a community, whether we like it or not, just because it is there; we have not thought about it, we have not produced it, except subconsciously perhaps, by actions about which we did not reflect or the consequences of which we did not calculate, and we are not positively aware of its existence or personally interested in it. But there is that solidarity. And I call *subjective solidarity* the solidarity which we feel and create by an active attitude of our mind and soul.

The elements of objective solidarity in a nation—I do not pretend to exhaust them; there are many, but I will give some as examples of what I mean—are, in the first place, the territory, which is more or less like the cup of the community, the recipient in which the community pours itself and the shape of which, the color of which, and the movement of which, it takes. This location of the community gives it first its material existence and then quite a number of characteristics, all that is known as *local* characteristics and which make it easy to distinguish a certain flavor, a certain manner of being, between one community and another.

Under this general heading we might, of course, include all that goes under climate, atmosphere, habitat, and so forth.

The second element of objective solidarity is the dependence on common means of supply; because after being, after the perfectly innocent and primitive fact of being, there comes the necessity of subsisting. And a community generally is tied into a solidarity by the feeling that all the members of it depend on the same means of supply.

The third element is the interdependence created between the members of a community by the machinery of civilization. Now, this is a very important element in our present-day solidarity and one which has grown considerably during the last century or so, because in the old days, and even nowadays, if a man so wishes, in some parts of the world, even in this country, a man can isolate himself and play the Robinson Crusoe. I do not believe that Robinson Crusoe himself was altogether without a society behind him; he had his tools that he had taken from the ship; he had his remembrances, he had his thoughts, he had quite a considerable education received from the society to which he had belonged, and therefore I do not imply that it is possible for a man to cut himself off altogether from a community. That is, of course, an absolute impossibility. Still we can conceive, even today, and it was quite a general case in the old days, say a hundred years ago, the case of people who constituted a tiny community, say a family or even one individual, completely isolated because their wants were reduced to such an extent that they need not rely on the supply received from centers outside their own. But nowadays most of us have so far developed our needs, which we receive from organized and mechanized communities, that we are fast becoming pieces of that machinery which brings to our house every day and every hour the necessities that we have made *our* necessities—such as light, heat, gas, electricity, water, and even our daily opinions that are served to us every morning in our newspaper.

There is no question that this solidarity, this increased mechanical solidarity, is having a great effect on us from the international point of view, and when I have dealt with the contrast between it and subjective solidarity I shall have to refer to this point again. But I want to point out to you that another most important element of solidarity is the feeling of common danger. There is one typical case in history in which a community has been blended together entirely, or almost entirely, by the feeling of common danger, in the absence of the other usual ties which bind communities together—except that of territory. I refer, of course, to Switzerland. Switzerland has three or four languages. It has several religions—I do not know how many. It has certainly no united culture in the deepest sense of the word. But Switzerland is a very resistant and a very closely knit community, and this is due to the feeling of common danger which the Swiss derived from the fact that these sturdy Swiss, keen on their liberty, lived in the midst of Europe, surrounded by three very important, powerful, and ambitious communities—Germany, Italy, and France. Here is a case, a very clear case of solidarity through danger.

A strong feeling of solidarity comes from blood, the

community of blood—by which I do not mean a community of race, because a pure race is, fortunately, a fact almost unknown in the world and probably would be strongly linked up with stupidity. The more I observe Europe the more I am convinced that one of the reasons why the European Continent has excelled in intellect is that it is one of the most mixed continents in the world. The nations of Europe united by a common blood feeling are not united because they belong to only one race but because they have been intermarrying for a long time and have attained a certain amount of interbreeding which has made of them not a race in the biological sense of the word but, as one might say, rather a kind of enlarged united family. And that is also a strong element of solidarity, since there is a kind of family memory transmitted in the blood, and therefore a tendency to produce the same reactions in the same situations, and therefore a tendency toward internal harmony which points the way to solidarity in action.

This links up the solidarity of the blood with the solidarity of habits, which is also powerful in all people that have lived long together. There is a Spanish proverb, a rather homely proverb, about man and wife which says that people who have slept for long years on the same bed end in being of the same opinion; and very often it has been observed that people, even though they do not belong to the same family, who have lived for forty or fifty years in the same home take on in the end the features of the family within which they have lived for so long, if only because there is an inward sculpturing of the face and body by the spirit, and the spirit, being the same and doing the same gestures every day, and living in the same atmosphere, ends in shaping the face and body in more or less similar fashion.

Finally, there is also the solidarity of language. Whether language was given man so that he could hide his thoughts or manifest them, if only because, having the same language, human beings will develop the same way of doing either, evidently language is a powerful element of solidarity, particularly as it is the best and the easiest way of communicating. Language is the neutral solvent of the things that happen inside of men's minds. It goes in and out of all the minds of a community and makes them alive.

But, even when all these elements that I have enumerated, and those I have forgotten, are present and active in a community, the community cannot be said actually to exist unless it is conscious of itself. Therefore, no amount of objective solidarity is going to enable us to live in a community if we do not think and want it to be a community. The most beautiful example of subjective solidarity is that of Thomas More, who, seeing the criminal pass toward his death, exclaimed, "There but for the Grace of God goes Thomas More." The sense, the active sense that is in us that the other man is us, is only another form of us, is somebody that we might have been if we had happened to be in the circumstance in which he is; or because we may, because of the position we occupy in life, be in part responsible for the fact that that man is taken to his death as a murderer. This feeling of positive, effective, and intellectual solidarity as between man and man, once it rises to the comprehension of the organic character of the community which has all these objective characteristics to be a community but does not know itself to be a community, this feeling it is which on the day it lives in a sufficient number of its members, creates the community and elevates it to real existence.

Of course it is evident that while our national communities have risen to this stage, the world community has not. It is evident that most of the elements of objective solidarity are already active in the world community; and that some will never be attained, nor do we need to long after them, because they are not necessary. For instance, we do not expect the world community ever to attain the element of solidarity which is in language; the idea of a universal language is a will-o'-the-wisp. The most that we can attain is either an artificial language to link together a small number of human beings that may be able to master it, or, more likely, the use of one or two of the great languages of the world. Probably English will be the chosen one, and, as I was told in California by an internationally minded Dutchman, it may be that "American English" is becoming the language of the future. But the idea that the fifteen hundred millions of the world, with all their different ways of living and their different rhythms and different form of the throat and palate, are going to speak one day the same language is so mad that it is not necessary to discuss it.

Nevertheless, a common language is not a necessity; even though it figures as one of the elements in most communities it is not a necessity for the world community; and if a proof were wanted I would recall the fact that one of the smallest national communities that exist, and the strongest, Switzerland, has three or four national languages.

Nor do we want or expect that the world community is going to attain a solidarity due to blood. The idea of mixing the races is, in my opinion, deplorable. While the mixture of strains of the same color is positive, creative, productive, and to be encouraged, the mixture of different races, wholesale at any rate, is a capital mistake and has always been followed by disastrous results; therefore, that again is to be brushed aside as irrelevant to the question of the future of the world community which, far from lying in the mixing of its colors, on the contrary is to derive most of its interesting characteristics and of its creativeness from the fact that we shall be able to develop within the planet five or six different, entirely different, civilizations by respecting the idiosyncrasies of each of the several colors of the human race.

Therefore, without going right through all the list of the elements of objective solidarity we do not need to require any of them as essential, but we do observe that there are a sufficient number of them to have created in the world what we might call a potential world community, which is only awaiting its consciousness, that is to say the attaining of its subjective solidarity, in order to exist. Now it is necessary that I should at any rate, without discussing those that I do not consider as necessary, discuss some of the aspects of world solidarity which are essential in the constitution of the world community.

The first of them is that mechanical solidarity which we saw playing so important a rôle in the modern world. If you happen to be traveling in a car on one of the roads near New York, or for the matter of that, near Philadelphia, on a Sunday afternoon, having a fleet of cars before you and a fleet of cars behind you, and still another fleet of cars coming in the opposite direction next to you, you may be as haughty and proud as a maharajah, and you may be as rich as a California newspaper owner, but you will be bound to behave according exactly to the same mechanical laws as a drop of water in a pipe—save that the drop of water in a pipe does not get hot with bad temper. That is what I call objective solidarity, because you are there like an object, like a thing; in spite of all your pride as a human being, in spite of all the divine spark in you, you are a thing, an object, and that is exactly the position in which you are if, when you arrive in your house and turn on the switch, the light does not shine, because there is no electricity in the main. You are the servant, you are the slave of a huge mechanism of which you happen to be a piece.

The immense progress that mechanical invention has achieved in the last hundred years has greatly increased this solidarity, but with most remarkable positive, as well as negative, results. The positive results are those that are derived from the rapidity of material and mental communications, for evidently these two aspects of the progress of mechanical and electrical appliances have reduced what we might call the virtual size of the world. If we measure the world by putting one yardstick after another yardstick, that may be useful for some purposes but it is not a very interesting political measurement— except for gerrymandering. If we really want to get a good political measure of the world, we must apply one or other of these two yardsticks: the time it takes for a man, or for his goods, to go from one point of the world to another, and the time that it takes for the thought of man, for the news, for the views, for the opinions and for the emotions which these opinions develop, to go from one point of the world to another. That being so, if we apply the first criterion, the time it takes for a man to go from one point of the world to another, we find that the world today is about the size that France was in the time of Napoleon. And if we apply the second, the time it takes for an opinion, a view, a speech, an emotion, to travel from one point of the world to another and be known, the world is today about the size of the agora of Athens in the time of Pericles.

Now there is a law of natural expansion in man which makes him fill up with his activity all the space at his disposal. Evidently, when the world has become virtually smaller in this way he has filled it up just as in the older days he has filled up his nation and his city; and today, no businessman that is worth his salt does business only within his neighborhood, he does it with as much of the world as he has strength for; and no man is worthy of his salt who is content with reading the news about his country or town—he reads the news of the whole world. And one morning you are going to read about the news of the other ends of the world; in the afternoon you are going to enjoy a sonata of Beethoven; and in the evening hear by radio about events happening in Germany or reading by the side of your fire your Shakespeare or your Tolstoy. The result is that mentally and morally, as well as mechanically and materially, we have become members of the whole world.

Now it may be asked: Is not that mental and moral association with the rest of the world subjective solidarity? Not yet, because we are not *aware* of it and possibly we do not want it. It may be, and I know many people of that kind—and I am sure that you know many of them—who, although they are living in the world, do not like the world because they find that the world is too full of foreigners. And so it is. They only want one tiny step forward to become world citizens, they only want to realize that there are nothing but foreigners in the world.

Nor is the element of danger absent. Far from it. No foreign nation, of course, can attack the world commonwealth, which includes them all; Mars is not yet near enough, at least as a planet. But as a spirit, as the spirit of war, Mars is the enemy which threatens our world community and slowly creates or contributes to creating its objective solidarity. If there were again a world war, we should all suffer untold and incalculable misery.

The next step whereby our world community will become a world commonwealth is the attainment of subjective solidarity. Everything in life is achieved by the collaboration of things with man and man with things. Now, things have played the game; man is not ready yet. And what is it that keeps man from achieving this victory, from completing that which is lacking for bringing forth into the world that world community which, so far as *things* are concerned, is already there waiting for us?

### SOVEREIGNTY

The answer is national sovereignty. I am not going to deal with sovereignty now from the legal point of view, even though I may have to refer to it in a minute; I am going to deal with sovereignty in so far as sovereignty is a collective force, one of those moral forces which is immoral. What is sovereignty from that point of view? *It is a tendency, both primary and reactive, to consider or to assert the national will as the sole, or at least as the final, determinant of action.* As you see, I put forward a definition which does not tally, or does not coincide, has little to do with, the legal and juridical definition—an entirely different aspect of it. I am dealing with politics, that is to say with the mechanics of collective forces, and therefore I am taking sovereignty as a force and not as a legal idea. It is a living tendency and, of course, as no one has ever seen a nation and in fact there are only human beings, this tendency lives in human beings and, for practical purposes, manifests itself in the particular individuals who happen at the time to incarnate the power of the community as instituted in the State.

It follows that sovereignty as a collective force depends on the men at the helm, and on the other collective forces determined by the feeling of sovereignty as felt by the active citizens, and on the capacity that these active citizens have to transmit their pressure to the men at the helm.

The elements that may be observed in this collective force of sovereignty are many. One of them is that juridical *idea* to which I referred a minute ago. The fact that sovereignty has been established in the hearts of civilized Western people and, through them, of the Easterners, is due to the fact that, at some time in Europe, the *idea* of sovereignty, as a result of the decomposition of the Holy Roman Empire, came to be one of the most generally admitted juridical traditions in European nations. And even though this idea was then in most cases attached not to the State nor to the people but to the prince, the process of democratization of political ideas in the national field handed all the powers of the prince to the people without in any way taking their absolute character from them, so that democracies, for all their democratic tendencies, are as absolute as kings. Sovereignty therefore as an idea is today one of the elements which go to the formation and to the vivification of sovereignty as a collective force.

The second element is a psychological reaction which is very generally, is in fact, I should say, nearly universal, due to the fact that subjective solidarity is stronger within the area of the nation than beyond that area; in fact, it is only strong today *within* the area of the nation since it does not yet live in the wider area of the world. It follows that the frontiers are like deep gashes in collective solidarity, and until we fill up these gashes, until we fill up these ditches in the solidarity of human beings, we cannot expect the world to attain the subjective solidarity.

It is here that we observe the reason why sovereignty is an obstacle, and a serious obstacle, to the appearance or to the birth of world solidarity. It is because when the human being of any one nation reaches his frontier mentally, at that point his solidarity ceases; he finds himself in an entirely different atmosphere and he reacts in an entirely different way. Now this is a most interesting and living element. It is observable by all psychologists, and it should be analyzed and receive more attention than, to my knowledge, it has received. This *spontaneous* element of solidarity, of subjective solidarity, among the members of the same nation, even though they may have entirely different views of politics, never extends to the foreigner; so that if there is a mixed group of people holding a conversation on a subject of vital and contemporary interest about international affairs, the tone will change, the area of confidence will shrink, the things that will be said will not be the same so soon as the foreign elements have disappeared and the nationals find themselves alone. This is one of the facts of collective life. It is there. It is no good omitting it, we must count on it when we analyze what is happening, and it is fundamental in what goes on in the realm of world affairs which we are studying together.

Another most important element among those which constitute sovereignty as a force is an instinctive projection that all nationals make of their nation on the plane of ideals. Every nation, for its own citizens, with some exceptions, is idealized. We often observe in practically every nation the reaction against idealization. There are people who do not rest unless they revile their own nation. But it is really the same phenomenon. It is a natural reaction which seeks relief from the mass feeling of the national community. But the normal and primary fact is that nationals idealize their nation; often it occurs that, according to a psychological law which is perfectly well known in individual psychology, this idealization of the national community takes place along the most unexpected and absurd line, so that in some cases a national character might be accurately drawn taking the opinion that the nation has of itself and turning it upside down; for, by a kind of instinct, the national compensates on an idealistic plane all that which subconsciously he perceives to be weak in his own nation.

Another element, and a most important one in the realm of sovereignty, is an obscure force, a subconscious force manifesting itself collectively but more especially in gifted individuals, not necessarily brain-gifted, but character-gifted, for the expansion or growth of the community in question. Just as in individuals there is an element of ambition which makes the individual invade wider and wider areas of the life that surrounds him, if he feels the vitality so to do, so when nations have a strong vitality, certain gifted individuals within them, who act as the instruments whereby this national tendency is manifested, carry physically or mentally or financially or economically outside the frontiers of the nation the power, the personality, and the character of the nation in question.

This tendency to expansion may be spontaneous; it may be spontaneous in nations that have a strong vitality and are, often, quite subconscious about it. It is less spontaneous in others, who develop in this way more through the stimulus of imitation or by history or by example. For instance, there is no doubt that the majesty and power of the British Empire—even though peacefully enjoyed by its nationals, even though they may have cured themselves of any tendency to further expansion, to further acquisition—by its mere existence as an example of a successful expansion of an imperial people, has disastrous effects on what we might describe as *leaner* nations.

This element, the tendency to expansion, through the action of a mere blind vital force, or through a force more difficult to control when the imagination is hungry, is having today a deplorable effect on international affairs, and is one which is extremely difficult to handle fairly and justly.

And finally, there is one element which we must never forget to mention whenever there is a question of collective forces. We should never forget that everything in life lives in individuals; even though the essence of it may be collective it has to be manifested, and nothing in life, no spirit in life, ever gets manifested except through individuals. Therefore there is in sovereignty an element, a very important element, sometimes overpowering, which is the particular color, tendency, gusto, which is given to sovereignty as a collective force by the man who happens to incarnate it. It is evident that in a good, calm, cold, wise old English Prime Minister sovereignty will have a different connotation, a different taste, a different manner than if it happens to incarnate in a lion tamer or in a serpent charmer, such as you find in certain more favored nations than Britain.

With this element, an all-important element, I finish the examination of the question of sovereignty in its essence. When we have the pleasure of meeting again—pleasure so far as I am concerned—I will deal with other elements in sovereignty which are no longer essential but are to sovereignty as adjectives are to a subject, elements that give it local character and allow us to see this plant of sovereignty, which is preventing the union of the world, in all the variety it takes when its roots grow into sinewy trunks and these trunks develop along frontiers, according to the climates and the ways of these several nations and frontiers.

## II

# PSYCHOLOGICAL FACTORS
# IN INTERNATIONAL
# RELATIONS

BEFORE we come to the psychological factors which modify the essence of the moral or collective force we call sovereignty, let us pause a while on the question of its intensity: What is it that constitutes the intensity with which this force, sovereignty, acts in the field of forces that is the world community?

Now, the intensity of sovereignty does not differ from the intensity of any other force. The intensity with which a force is felt is made up of two factors: one is the inherent power within the force; the other one is the ability with which that power is wielded. The intensity of sovereignty, therefore, will depend on two factors: the inherent force of sovereignty, and the ability with which that force is wielded, or what possibly a mechanical engineer would call *its efficiency*. I should like to examine, successively, these two elements, because both are important in world life.

First as to the inherent power of a nation—apart, let me repeat, from the ability or efficiency with which it is wielded; the inherent power of a nation manifests itself, first, in the guise of such obvious things as the army, the navy, and the air force. A nation from the point of view of its inherent force is generally estimated in the public eye according to whether she possesses one hundred thousand, a million, or five million men. Similarly as to the tonnage of the navy; similarly about the number or power of its airplanes capable of bombing, chasing, or otherwise performing a military activity.

Now this is rather a symptomatic than an essential estimate, for it is evident—it is indeed a truism—that the inherent force of the nation is merely manifested in these forms of power which are its army, its navy, and its air force. It is not there itself. It is the cause of these things; it is not these things themselves. The cause can be traced back from these external appearances to something already more substantial, though not yet quite essential, namely, the economic and financial strength of the nation concerned; for evidently it is only on economic and financial strength that an army, navy, and air force can be efficiently evolved and possessed.

But even this second stage in our analysis of the inherent force of a nation does not go deep enough, and we have to consider now the elements that constitute the force of a nation as manifested, first, in its financial and economic strength or power, and then in its military, naval, and air power.

The first element is mass. If we compare two nations, such as China and Switzerland, we shall at once realize that mass is not an all-powerful element in the estimate of the force of a nation. There is something else than mass. But if you compare Switzerland and the United States you come back at once to realizing that all the same and in spite of your first observation, mass does count. What is then, exactly, the law that emerges from this double comparison, of China and Switzerland on the one hand and Switzerland and the United States on the other? It is that *all things being equal,* as the mathematicians say, the mass does count. I would even go so far as to say that in certain conditions and when the mass is really overwhelming, it is by its sheer presence already an important element in power.

May I draw here on a personal recollection? During the Manchurian question, we were once gathered—the members of the Council, except the parties—by Aristide Briand, in his rooms in the Hotel des Bergnes, in Geneva, for a free and informal discussion. In the course of this gathering, the French Prime Minister and Foreign Secretary, with his inimitable wit and humor, told us he had received the Japanese Ambassador and had said to him, "Mr. Ambassador, I have a friend who is a boxer. He is a very hefty man, a very strong man, and my friend the boxer tells me, 'Well, Mr. Le President, I am afraid of nobody; but I am afraid of a quilt, because I go for the quilt and strike at it with all the might of my fists and the quilt doesn't care at all and I just get tired.' Well, Mr. Ambassador, China is a quilt."

And all that has happened since shows the wisdom of the image struck by the French statesman; the mere fact of mass is already, in itself, an important element of power, of inherent force in the sovereignty of the nation if only because that mass can react in that very efficient way in which its own inertia enables it to react, by passivity. You all remember the enormous effect which the mere mass and distance of Russia produced on the Napoleonic campaigns.

Yet mass of course is not, in spite of all this, the fundamental element in the inherent power of a nation, as shown by the example of very small nations like Belgium and Switzerland, who wield a considerable economic and financial power in spite of their very exiguous mass. What is this, then, due to? It is mostly due to technical capacity, ability, brain-ability, for organizing and leading human beings in the mastering and the controlling of the forces of nature. It is mostly attained through intellectual capacity for the physical, chemical, and mathematical sciences, as well as in the sciences and practical arts of administration and government. This is a force in itself; we need no other definition, and it acts like a powerful factor in the inherent power of a nation.

The next element of power is social discipline; not altogether unconnected with the second, for wherever you find in human beings that technical capacity for controlling the forces of nature, and also for controlling the discoveries of science and even leading them, in which we have seen the second element of power, it generally goes with a predominance of reason over other faculties of the human soul, and therefore an easier coördination of effort in the members of the community, a greater capacity for analyzing events without violence, and consequently the possibility of coördinating all the forces of the community—mass forces and intellectual forces—and enables the government to wield them more firmly in its own hand. With this virtue is very strongly connected the element of patriotism, about which I do not think it is necessary for me to enlarge any further.

So, when closely analyzed, this somewhat dramatic appearance of force, as manifested in the armies, the navies, and the air forces of nations, resolves itself into an individual capacity in the members of those nations for reaching a balance, a government of themselves and of their human relations by reason, excluding violence and therefore a well-organized series of virtues, beginning with the right government of personal affairs which enables the accumulation of financial and economic surpluses in banks, those banks gathering up these surpluses, administering them with wisdom and intelligence, and building up a kind of structure of financial and economic stability which in the end has for its apex the government. The governments in their turn are generally intelligent, since they belong to these advanced nations who are advanced because they themselves are intelligent and technically capable; but moreover, they find already a good deal or most of their work done for them by the fact that the nations which they govern are spontaneously well balanced and well organized. So that they have the immense advantage of possessing in their hand an instrument of force consisting of an element of mass, multiplied by an element of ability.

Quite apart from this inherent force, the ability to wield that force is a most important element toward our estimate of sovereignty. It is evident that the political ability to wield the inherent power of the nation enters already as one of the elements of the inherent force of the nation, since we have admitted—we have indeed put forward—the view that a good deal of this inherent force results from the political capacity of the nation in general to organize itself into a well-built construction of financial, economic, and political forces. But it enters also as a very important element *outside of it,* as a kind of coefficient of efficiency in the manipulation of this force in external affairs. We would then say that political ability for internal affairs is an element of the inherent force of a nation, while political ability for external affairs is a coefficient, and multiplies this inherent force and gives it its efficiency. The coefficient may, as all who have studied arithmetic know, be greater than the unit or lesser than the unit; that is to say, it may increase the inherent force of the nation, or it may decrease it if the political ability for external affairs is not as high as the political ability for internal affairs.

For, and this is a very important point, it does not follow that when a nation has political ability for internal affairs it has an equal amount of it for external affairs. To be sure, certainly it will not be politically stupid for external affairs, for it is not conceivable that ability should altogether change its sign when crossing the frontier; but there are elements in the management of world affairs outside the frontiers of a nation that do not obtain in the management of affairs inside the national frontiers, and therefore it is quite easy to imagine that a government may be more capable of organizing its own inherent force than of wielding it efficiently in the foreign fields.

Without aiming at an exhaustive analysis of the elements that enter into this ability for external affairs, we may enumerate some of them. To begin with, there is a very important element in the knowledge of what is going on, or in other words, in accurate and up-to-date information. Most of the great Powers possess that information as a matter of course. They have the means, the financial means to pay for a sufficient number of foreign representatives, either avowed, such as consuls, or not avowed—they have another name which it is neither necessary nor polite to quote—and these people keep their governments posted with what really is going on.

This factor of accurate information gives to the great powers a tremendous advantage over lesser nations. Take anything that happens in the world nowadays; take, for instance, the Manchurian question; take the Abyssinian question. When the members of the Council gathered in Geneva or Paris or London to discuss these questions, the position of the members of the great Powers who had abundant reports as to what had happened or was going to happen, as to who was who and why he was there, as to the exact financial, economic, political, military background, those members had a considerable advantage over the members of the Council who, belonging to smaller nations, did not possess this accurate and complete information. Here is then an element of efficiency in the wielding of sovereignty in which can at once be seen the considerable difference there is between the big nations and the small nations.

The second element is the capacity for acquiring an adequate knowledge of persons, a knowledge of the persons with whom foreign affairs are actually transacted. This in its turn in great part depends on the knowledge of foreign languages and of foreign cultures, that is to say, on the number of foreign-traveled people at the disposal of the nation in question—that is, foreign-traveled *and* capable of profiting by travel, for there is nothing more traveled than a good portmanteau or trunk, and yet it does not gather much knowledge of foreign people. This assumes that foreign-traveled human beings must be able to see with their eyes and to see with their intellect, and to gather their own conclusions. But not even good observation powers, nor even a good intelligence will be of much avail if behind the people used in foreign employ there is not a sound general outlook, and particularly a sound world culture. The people who are sent abroad— not to *lie* for their country, as runs the famous definition of ambassadors—but to work for the country, must be in a position to pick up what is happening and refer it to a general outlook, a general culture, to what the Germans would call a *Weltanschauung,* which is enlightened and really substantial, so that the observations made refer and coördinate in an harmonious whole.

Finally, a very important element in the control of foreign affairs in the ability to wield the internal force of the nation for foreign purposes is a supply of masterful individuals. Now, masterful individuals cannot be made by machinery. They appear, or they do not appear. They are a kind of person about whom every nation is bound to remain in a kind of Mr. Micawber state of mind, expecting that they will turn up. But here again, we find how un-favored small nations are in comparison with big nations. For it is obvious that a nation with a considerable amount of economic and financial power and with a considerable amount of military power—many soldiers and much ton-nage and many airplanes—can, more easily than less de-veloped nations, afford to have a stupid foreign secretary.

Such is then, in outline, what can be said of the inten-sity of sovereignty. We have now discussed the essence of sovereignty and the intensity of sovereignty. If I insist on the characteristics of sovereignty, it is because I am sure we all agree that in the whole field of forces of the world community, sovereignty is far and away the most im-portant.

### PSYCHOLOGICAL FACTORS WHICH MODIFY SOVEREIGNTY

Up to now we have been considering sovereignty in the abstract, and it might be good if now we ventured on a more delicate ground and tried to see it working in the actual sphere in which it is bound to work—in the sphere of human relationships, human tensions, historical rela-tions and historical traditions, and see how this idea of sovereignty—up to the present, general and abstract—qualifies itself, takes color, under the influence of psychological factors, namely, how the psychological relations between the nations of the world community influence the practical application of the principle, of the emotion, and of the primary force of sovereignty.

Politics belong eminently to the realm of action and we are in an eminently political age—possibly getting out of it now but certainly still within it; for it is a curious thing and a remarkable thing in the history of the West that at every moment of this history the nations that have occupied the forefront of the stage have not been chosen by a kind capricious spirit in an irresponsible way. It may perhaps be suggested that at every given time, that particular nation has taken the main rôle which at the moment represented the spirit of the times with greatest fidelity; at every given moment of modern history one particular tendency in human civilization took the main position, and that nation which in a permanent way represents that position automatically came to the fore, by a kind of historical "resonance." It acquired a greater importance because it happened to be at the time the nation more directly representative of the spirit of the time.

In the sixteenth century, the main object of people's thoughts and emotions was the life beyond—what was to happen to the human soul once it left this earth—the sixteenth century was eminently the century of religion; it was therefore but natural that Spain should take the main rôle because Spain has always been interested in absolute principles, in the dogmatism of absolute principles; and even today, the main explanation of the civil war in Spain is not to be found in this or that claim, of this or that class; it is to be found in the absolute incompatibility of two absolute dogmatic positions.

Similarly, when the religious question is settled and the

world settles down to an examination of the rational way of living in this earth and to an analysis of a way of balancing individual claims in our western civilization, the nation that comes to the fore is France, the rationalistic nation, the nation which all through the eighteenth century lays down the foundations of the rationalistic era and establishes the philosophical principles of what was to become the French Revolution, and, in the end, the liberal democracies of the nineteenth century.

But when again that political question is settled and, under the lee of political liberty there occurs the splendid blossoming out of economic activities, and, under the facilities afforded by the principle of every man for himself, progress takes place at an unprecedented rate at the beginning of the first half of the nineteenth century, then England, the nation of action, comes to the fore; we are then in the English period, the period of the nineteenth century, because England represents then, more characteristically than any other nation, the spirit of the epoch. Finally, it is not through any hazard that the United States of America came to the fore immediately after the War, because it was the natural outcome of the mechanistic age; it is characteristic of this nation as shown, for instance, even in the trends of its psychological studies—its typically psychological studies, not the foreign imported—that it lays a stress on the mechanical operation of life and thus, with the progress of the mechanical era, the United States of America comes to the fore.

It is quite possible that we may be on the eve of yet another transition which is announced by the evident popularity of all that pertains to Russia. That is a matter for the immediate future, and we should not venture to analyze the future; it is bold enough for us to analyze the past and the present, but we can hardly fail to observe that, with the change of the age, a change of supremacy, of leadership in the nations may probably be dictated by a change in the general trends of humanity in general.

At present, however, we are still in the period of action, for the shift of supremacy between England and America is not fundamental, it is only adjective. Action is still the basis of our life, even though it may be more organic in England, more mechanical in America. Action is the law of the period, and as a result of it the greatest prestige goes to the peoples of action. It follows that the peoples of action, rationally or irrationally, intellectually or instinctively, tend to underestimate the peoples who do not follow their way of living; and as a result of it there is a psychological tension which, from the point of view of the peoples of action, tends to encourage them to launch into a period of expansion and to experience a feeling of extraordinary health and power. It is, therefore, natural that at the present stage we should still be in a period of predominance of England, and of great development for the United States of America.

Strange as it may seem for persons immersed in this period, this has not been so always. We are so used to this era of admiration and imitation of action, of the peoples who succeed in the realm of action, that we have difficulty to imagine other points of view. But two very curious and, in fact, amusing examples pertaining to the psychological relations between England and Spain come to my memory. When, at the beginning of the seventeenth century, Charles I of England went to Spain with Buckingham in order to woo the Infanta of Spain, the impression which these two English noblemen made on the grave Spaniards was that of a shocking lack of dignity; because, on the slightest pretext, they danced about and gesticulated in a manner quite unworthy of a gentleman. When again, at a later stage in the eighteenth century, Father Feijóo, a famous Spanish Jesuit, an intellectualist and one of the leaders of eighteenth-century thought in Spain, discussing Shakespeare, whose work he knew very well as he knew Bacon's, explains to the Spaniards that the reason why Shakespeare's plays always end in such terrific slaughter is that the English are a bloodthirsty nation, a cruel nation, and that this is due to their diet excessively high in meat. I myself, as Minister of Education, forbade by decree of the Republic the use of a Manual of Contemporary History, then a textbook in three secondary schools of the country, in which it was said that the cause of the brutality of the English was the love of whiskey and rum. Worse things circulate about Spain in history textbooks current in this country.

This psychological relationship, to which I shall have to come back later, is no doubt one of the most important elements in the actual working of sovereignty in the present age; we all remember the extraordinary effect produced in the world when Italy dared stand up to Great Britain which, for a very long time, had succeeded in carrying on the affairs of the world in complete peace, owing to the fact that it was often quite sufficient for England to say "No" for things not to happen, and to say "Yes" for things to happen. This was entirely due to the accumulated capital of prestige obtained by England in a series of almost constant successes, due to the fact that she was the nation in harmony with the spirit of the time, which was the spirit of action.

A second example of the way in which psychology modifies the usual sovereignty may be found in the situation created in international affairs by the dissatisfaction of gifted peoples, who consider themselves below the rank which they, owing to their gifts, deserve. There are two— I would not perhaps say nations, but at any rate states— that figure prominently in this category: the German State and the Italian State. There is no question, when all is said for or against in the matter of war-guilt, that even in the great war of 1914 the German Nation challenged the world, owing to a certain feeling, independent of whose responsibility it was, but owing to a certain feeling that Germany did not wield in the world the power and the majesty and the importance which her undisputed mental ability, according to her own lights, enabled her to wield.

Evidently if the matter be examined more thoroughly, Germany was mistaken because, though the mental ability of the German Nation is probably unrivaled and it is at the center of mental talent in Europe and, therefore, in the world, possibly that talent is not political talent and, since what is wanted for the government of the world and for political expansion is specifically political talent, without going to fetch the other forms of talent upon which the English, for example, may be far inferior to the Germans, nevertheless the fact remains that at that time, rightly or wrongly—and again, now, rightly or wrongly—Germany, and also Italy, considered themselves in an inferior rank to that which in their eyes corresponds to their capacity; and that is a psychological element which, independently of whether we think it right or wrong, is objectively one of the important forces which tend to give color, tension, direction, and sense to the application of sovereignty in international affairs.

The same characteristics obtain with regard to Japan, whose psychological situation is even more delicate owing to the question of race. The question of racial relations be-

tween the Japanese and the Whites is well known so that it
would be impertinent to press this point home any further;
but it is evident that along with the feeling of injustice due
to the realization, rightly or wrongly, the subjective feeling that Japan has not yet obtained in the world the rank
which corresponds to her eminence in other walks of life,
along with that feeling, common with Italy and Germany,
there is a new element complicating matters with regard to
Japan, due to the difficulty arising out of the racial relation.

Now this dissatisfaction, which is a thing in itself, what
we might call a pure state of mind, a purely subjective state
of mind, is complicated by the fact that there is in history
a phenomenon called imperial expansion which has, or
seems to have—for it is difficult to generalize—but seems to
have a well-known cycle of expansion, fulfillment, and in-
volution; and that the several nations that we have been
discussing happened to be in different stages in this cycle.
Here, with regard to the phase of the imperial cycle, the
most advanced nation is Spain. Spain conquered this Continent, civilized it, colonized it, organized it and lived in
it peacefully—and that is very often forgotten—during three
centuries, and at the end of those centuries the usual thing
happened; the nations that Spain had created were too
grown up to consent any more to her rule. They seceded
from Spain and the cycle is over. Spain is no longer in this
Continent, and the imperial cycle of the country is closed.

Behind Spain in the imperial evolution comes England;
whose imperial evolution is well-nigh closed in all that
concerns the Dominions; but, as England has been so active during the last two centuries, one might say that her
imperial cycle is complex—closed in respect to one part of
her Empire, still proceeding and developing with regard to

other parts of it; nevertheless England is probably, after Spain, the most advanced nation in her imperial experience, to such an extent that you may already perceive in some Englishmen the feeling that Spain well knows, i. e., that empires, so far as England is concerned, are of the past. France, Holland, and Portugal are in similar periods to that of England, more or less advanced, according to this or that territory in their development. But there are nations whose empires are still green, are still in the future. There is Japan, there is Italy, there is Germany. And this imperial tradition, about which we know not whether it is going to be historically closed for every nation, with the growth of new ideas on the organic solution of the world community, or whether it is going to proceed in the old historical way by means of international wars— this phenomenon of empire development which history teaches us is evidently creating very strong psychological tensions which happen to work along with those of my preceding series—those arising out of the dissatisfied nations on their own merits.

Germany, Italy, Japan feel not only dissatisfied in themselves, because they believe themselves higher and more capable than the world seems to realize, but also feel that in the historical process of empire development they have been caught by events at a moment when they were justified in expecting an equal career to that obtained by the other nations before them. Not unfairly, one might put the position of Germany and Italy and Japan toward the League of Nations as that of the gambler who, having seen one or two gamblers making huge amounts of money during the night, would then listen to them getting up and pulling a very long face, and saying, "Gentlemen, gambling is a very ugly vice; we must wind up."

There are still quite a number of other psychological factors in world affairs arising out of what we might describe as moral empires. For instance, one of the most curious psychological relationships in Europe today is an underground, never-spoken-of rivalry between France and Italy for the supremacy of the Latin world. France claims that supremacy on the ground of her intellectual achievements and a long history of intellectual leadership; Italy, on the ground of a history which, from the intellectual point of view, is no less illustrious if perhaps older, and also on the fact that she happens to be built around Rome.

This is an insoluble problem; it is absolutely impossible to solve a rivalry between these two nations for the leadership of the Latin world. The fact remains that so far, of the people who learn another language than their own, most people of the Latin world learn French rather than Italian, probably under the delusion that Italian need not be learned in order to be spoken, which is one of the great delusions in international affairs. And it would be very difficult to exaggerate the extent to which this factor—having nothing to do with economics and very little to do with politics, strictly speaking—complicates international affairs. It is seldom referred to. It is there all the time, and it turns up in the oddest places. For instance, the commission appointed for examining the suggestions made by architects for the new building for the League of Nations in Geneva found it absolutely necessary that French and Italian architects should receive prizes—otherwise, who knows what a catastrophe might have ensued.

France and Italy, therefore, feel instinctively that there is a moral empire there for them to lead. And it is a very similar position—though a quite immaterial position, in reality, quite a noble ambition in itself because it does not seek any material advantage—but a very similar position to that created by the psychological complications of the development of territorial and colonial empires.

Now, there are three or four other situations of the kind. There is the undoubted ambition of Spain to maintain its leadership over the culture of South America. Considering that the material and territorial empire is gone, there remains what some Spanish rhetorical patriots call the empire of the culture and of the language. There it is for what it is worth. It is one of the psychological elements in international affairs. Its main force comes from the fact that Spain hardly ever makes use of it.

There is a similar situation, quite parallel, between England and the United States, in which England, in her very wise way and very quiet way, still maintains a desire to keep at any rate the cultural link with the United States of America, owing to the common origin of the language and culture.

And finally, a similar rivalry to that obtaining between France and Italy over the Latin world obtains between France and Germany over the whole world; the French genius and the German genius, the French *esprit* and the German *Kultur,* trying to get over the world a kind of kingship or queenship over the spirit, culture, of science, of the arts and, generally, of life in the whole world.

All these elements are more important in international affairs than appears at first sight. They tend to render world-relations delicate, complex, difficult to settle, in an irrational way, even when the more substantial and material elements that are in dispute have already been got out of the way.

I enter now on an even more difficult and delicate ground in this analysis of the psychological relationships which modify the use of sovereignty, by referring to yet another psychological factor very seldom found in political discussions—that which might be called *subconscious imitation*. I hold the view that most of the difficulties of Great Britain are due to imitators of Great Britain; or, in other words, that most of the enemies of Great Britain are imitators of Great Britain who do not realize to what extent they imitate her. For instance, the natural psychological position of the Irishman is to care very little for his nation and much more for his own free and unfettered life. The Irishmen—in reality, Spaniards who took the wrong trail and went north—the Irishmen are like all Spaniards, fundamental anarchists; but they lived under the sway of Great Britain for a long time—longer than they particularly liked —and as a result of it they have absorbed from Great Britain the other spirit, the spirit of subservience to the interests of the nation; and this conquest, the psychological conquest of Great Britain over the Irish soul, was the death knell of the political conquest of Great Britain over the Irish territory, because on the day that the Irish took on a political English psychology they became Sinn Feiners. Sinn Fein is Irish words with English music. It is the Nation; "We," that is to say, not *I* but *we,* and on the day that the nation says "We," on that day they are speaking English sense, even when they are speaking Irish words. The Irish Rebellion was psychologically an English affair.

And that is the first example of what England has done in many places in the world; for England is the most perfect nation there is, in the sense that England needs no outside authority, no outside discipline, no outside pressure to exist in every one of her Englishmen; and every foreigner with whom the English come into political contact realizes this, and emulates it—and becomes a better citizen! As, of course, England had the misfortune of coming into very intimate contact with Ireland, Ireland learned it first and was the first to revolt, as soon as she became a country of imitators of England.

The same thing happens in India. The Indian never had in his life the sense of nationalism. Nationalism is a western affair, mostly an English affair, and never interested the Indians until the English taught them. But when the Indian intellectuals realized what it was, how perfect an organization of life, of collective life, this English Nationalism is, then they were possessed by the desire to emulate the English, and of course they all became foes in the same process —because you may at the same time hate and imitate; in fact, very often imitating leads to hating and hating to imitating.

A similar case of imitation, in an entirely different field, naturally, since the model is different, occurs between Rumania and Poland on the one hand and France on the other. Rumania is a keen imitator of France, and Bucharest is never happier than when it is called the "Second Paris." Poland is a more complex case; the imitation of Rumania is straightforward and even if, politically, there is a reaction against it in the form of a pro-German Party, nevertheless there is no psychological reaction against the psychological fact, as such; while in Poland there is at the same time the feeling of imitation and the reaction of anti-imitation, because the Polish Nation has always been an extremely proud nation. As a result of it the Poles are ultra-nationalist; a desire to become a great power as a reaction to the fact that Poland has been twice obliterated from the map of Europe gives zest and vitality to the attitude of a defensive psychological feature in the existence of Poland. The contemporary history of Europe will immediately suggest abundant proofs of the effects of these psychological factors.

Then there is South America. In South America there are two main imitative tendencies—France and the United States. They imitate France in literature and the arts; they imitate the United States of America in politics. The immense majority of the South American constitutions are copied on the Constitution of this country, and I do not know whether I should be allowed to say that the ill effects of the Constitution in this country are multiplied by the fact that it suits the South American nations even less than it suits this country.

I come now to an even more difficult example of psychological factors, for we are ascending a painful gradient. I refer to what we might describe as the colonial complex. It afflicts the whole of this continent. There is a distinct colonial complex in the United States toward England. There are a number of people in this country who imitate the English and either love or hate them, or both at a time. Such people are often found amongst naval officers and diplomats of the United States of America. For instance, the very existence of the navy of America is purely an imitation of Great Britain. The immense power of this Nation needs no navy at all to make itself felt in the world! There is no harm in the American navy being there. I have nothing to say against it. The policy of having a navy, obviously, must be backed with a navy. But this republican and democratic country, if free from imitators of England, might have invented a policy that needed no navy. Unfortunately, the imitators of England had no imagination and decided that this immense and self-contained continent would have the same policy and the same navy as the little European island.

This state of mind is characteristic of the colonial nation. In psychology the relation between the colony and the mother country is very similar to the psychological relation between the mother and child or, rather, between child and mother. It is at the same time one of intimate love and of violent opposition, very often verging on hate. The situation is exactly the same, with differences introduced by racial characteristics, between the Spanish-American nations and Spain, save that here we meet with a further complication that comes to ride over the first idea—the idea of mere colonial relationship—namely, the fact that in Spanish America a considerable proportion of Indians have remained, of the original race that was beaten by the invader. This gives rise to more complicated relationships, because not only is there the same double complicated connection between the whites of the South American country and the mother country, which obtains in the United States toward England, but on top of that there is a psychological element of the beaten race toward the conqueror, and the fact that in many cases the two races have mixed and all these psychological tensions occur inside individual souls. This creates between South America and Spain an extraordinarily complicated set of forces which makes Spanish policy in South America extremely difficult. Because if Spain does not act, she risks being misrepresented, her passivity being misrepresented as neglect; and if Spain does act, her activity may be misrepresented as an obsolete tendency to rule her ex-colonies. And there is always the possibility of striking the wrong side of the situation, since it has the two tensions at the same time, the positive and the negative.

Finally, to end up with something a little less irritating, let us mention the element of international courtesy. Inter-

# III

# LIMITATIONS OF SOVEREIGNTY

### THE COVENANT AND SOVEREIGNTY

HAVING outlined sovereignty as a moral force, analyzed its intensity and provided some examples of the psychological forces which modify it, we must now proceed to a somewhat detailed study of the limitations which our contemporary international life imposes on sovereignty. And though perhaps this is not the most methodical way of going about it, it may be well to begin with the limitations brought to sovereignty by the Covenant of the League of Nations. Not a very good method, perhaps, in that the Covenant of the League of Nations brings to sovereignty a motley of limitations of different kinds; and it might perhaps be better to proceed logically, category by category. But on the other hand the Covenant is too important an instrument to be torn to tatters in the logical exposition of the theme; and we may gain the advantage of an excellent illustration of the way in which a living instrument can modify an international mental habit of so long and so rooted a standing as sovereignty.

The Covenant occupies in world life a very special position in that it is a *universal, permanent,* and *official* system for the linking together of the Nations of the world. And before we enter into the analysis of the ways in which it limits sovereignty, it may be useful to agree about these three points, none of which are, at first sight, quite evident. For it might be argued that the Covenant is not universal, and on no soil could this accusation be made more eloquently than on the soil of the United States of America which, being the most important nation in the world, has never belonged to the system founded by the Covenant.

## Universality of the Covenant

Yet this system is universal. Article I of the Covenant describes the original members of the League of Nations as "those of the signatories which are named in the Annex to this Covenant, and such of those other States named in the Annex as shall accede without reservation to this Covenant." This complicated and somewhat cryptic way of describing the members of the League of Nations was forced on the delegates by the political considerations of the time and the pressure of their public opinions. The French did not want Germany in; Wilson did not want Mexico in; and most of the nations of the world did not want Russia in. So that, legally speaking, diplomatically speaking, and even, at the time, politically speaking, the Covenant was not born universal, and the League was aptly named "League" and not "World Commonwealth," in that it really was an association, and a limited association, of states, chosen for considerations of alliance or association which were at the same time positive in that there was a certain amount of confidence and war comradeship between partners, and negative in that the Pact deliberately excluded from the partnership a certain number of states which for one reason or another one nation or another could not accept.

And yet everything that has happened since, even in spite of the deplored and deplorable absence of the United States, has done nothing but emphasize the spirit of universality of the Covenant. The thing was so inherent in the spirit of the time, the sense of universality of the world community seeking to become a world commonwealth was so strong, that speaker after speaker in the Assembly began from the first to put forward the plea of universality as if universality was legally inscribed in the Covenant, while as a matter of fact it is explicitly excluded from its text. It is one of those cases, and they are numerous in the history of the League, in which the spirit of the times went rapidly ahead of the letter of the times.

This plea of universality was first put forward by the Argentine, in the first Assembly. It even led to a withdrawal of the delegation on meeting with an unfavorable atmosphere. Then Monsieur Motta, the representative of Switzerland, asked in a later Assembly that Germany should be admitted, provoking one of the most eloquent and impassioned speeches that Geneva has heard from the lips of Monsieur Viviani, the French delegate. Yet, despite such opposition, the movement culminated in the entrance of Germany, as a result of which Geneva again heard one of the most moving and one of the most magnificent orations that ever a statesman gave to the world, in the speech with which Monsieur Briand admitted and received Germany into the League.

Later again, after Mexico had been excluded under pressure from Wilson, not precisely perhaps of his own accord but bound by a public opinion of this country, which in those days, as you may remember, was quite "oil-influenced" against Mexico, there was a famous Assembly in Geneva in which Spain and all the big Powers successively asked that Mexico should come into the League of Nations, on the plea of the universality of the League of Nations. And then again, in spite of every opposition in more recent times, in the name again of universality, the Union of Socialist Soviet Republics was admitted to the League of Nations with flying colors.

## Permanent Character of the Covenant

The Covenant is, therefore, more in the spirit than in the letter a universal instrument. It is also a permanent instrument. Article I, Paragraph 3, says that "Any member of the League may, after a two years' notice of his intention so to do, withdraw from the League, provided that all its international obligations and all its obligations under this Covenant shall have been fulfilled at the time of its withdrawal." And as you know, there are being repeated cases of withdrawal, as a consequence of violation. It is a curious example of the way in which reality evades theory and takes its own line; that while the drafters of the Covenant determined, in Article 16, Paragraph 4, that the League could always pronounce the *exclusion* of any of its members that violated its Covenant, this has never been applied, violation being, on the contrary, followed by the violent departure of the violator, who bangs the door without saying good-bye. But such is life; always unexpected.

Yet precisely, not so much because of but despite this, the Covenant is a permanent instrument. It is not an instrument which has an end at any time. Any one of its members may leave after two years' notice at any time that it feels that the house has become too strict for his behavior. But the whole, the altogether of the association is constant, and therefore we are in the presence of a permanent entity and therefore, we may add, in the presence of an institution.

## Official Character of the Covenant

Finally, this association is official. That is to say, it has all the characteristics of a state. It is useless and theoretical, in the bad sense of the word, to argue about whether the League is a super-state or a level state or an under-state; it is a state, if not an entity of the same species, in that it is official, an official institution, an association of states. It has, therefore, all the characteristics and all the dignity of a State.

We are in the presence then of a permanent institution, a political association of states or, what amounts to the same, an association of sovereignties, and as there is no association without limitation we are in the presence of a system for the limitation of sovereignties.

Hence, while it lasts—and it is very difficult to believe that it may altogether be dissolved—while it lasts, sovereignty is limited in time. It is also limited in area, and that is what I should like now to examine with you in some detail. But at the risk of committing an "Irish bull," I should like to begin this study of the limitations of sovereignty in the Covenant by pointing out to what an extent the Covenant does *not* limit sovereignty.

## Sovereignty Unlimited by the Covenant

To begin with, there are quite a number of provisions in the Covenant in virtue of which the sovereignty of the States members is fully reserved. Such is the case particularly of Article V, and of its necessary adjunct, Article IV, Paragraph 5. Article V decrees that all decisions taken by the Council and by the Assembly must be taken by the whole, by unanimity. Which means that any one state considers its own sovereignty as of sufficient importance to block the decisions taken by all the other states put together. This, from the point of view of the members, is inevitable. From that of the Association, it is absurd. And

in actual fact it is on that really absurd system that the
League is run. The fact that it is run under that absurd system is a sufficient proof of its vitality.

Article IV, Paragraph 5, completes the mischief by establishing on quite clear terms that whenever the Council
is dealing with a question that concerns any particular
Nation, deliberately and specifically, that Nation becomes
for the time being a member of the Council. And, although
often delegates of nations called to sit at the Council in
virtue of this provision address the Council as if they were
parties before a tribunal, it is merely a mistake of delegates—delegates do commit mistakes—because they do not
realize that they are full members of the Council with
exactly the same rights as the others to examine the case
which interests them, and that is why they are there.

Why are they there? Precisely because, since the Council
must act unanimously, and since it is acknowledged that
the particular question at issue is one that explicitly interests the nation in question, immediately the Covenant
acknowledges the right of that nation to become a member
of the Council for the time being, so that if necessary it
can put its sovereignty in the balance and block the pro-
ceedings.

This again is inevitable. But for seventeen years the
League of Nations has been run on this system, and yet
though the Assembly, which votes the budget of the League
of Nations, has to vote it unanimously every year, the
League has never lacked its budget. Which nation would
have been sure of having its budget voted if its parliament
had to vote it by a unanimous vote! A striking proof of
the vitality of the world commonwealth since, in spite of
the rule of unanimity, at no moment has the Assembly
been unable to vote a budget in the extremely short period

left for its discussion, about two to three weeks at the most.

This does not mean—far from it—that the rule of unanimity is a healthy rule, even when it is reasonably applied. In recent times, and particularly since the Manchurian question, there has developed in the League of Nations, even in the most authoritative circles of the League, a tendency to exaggerate the rule of unanimity beyond common sense. For a long time some of us have had, in Geneva, a permanent argument with eminent jurists; we asserted that common sense is a rule of law, which eminent jurists denied.

Lest I be suspected of exaggeration, I want to draw your attention to Article X. Article X says that "The members of the League undertake to respect and preserve as against external aggression the territory, integrity, and existing independence of all members of the League. In case of any such aggression, or in case of any threat or danger of such aggression, the Council shall advise upon the means upon which this obligation shall be fulfilled."

Now, before we know whether Article X is applicable, we must know whether there has been external aggression against the territorial integrity and the existing political independence of a member of the League. And eminent jurists used to tell us in Geneva that if you argue that State A has committed such an aggression, the question concerns that State A. In virtue of Article IV, Paragraph 5, that State becomes for the time being a member of the Council. In virtue of Article V, the Council votes unanimously, and that suspected member votes, which of course means that it votes that no such aggression exists. Ergo, Article X cannot be applied. A beautiful construction, but it assumed that common sense is not a rule of law.

Now, we maintain that common sense is a rule of law

and that, therefore, the rule of unanimity should not apply to Article X, or else it destroys the value of the article altogether. But an equally bad and possibly a worse case occurs in relation to Article XI. After all, Article X has always remained somewhat under a shadow, owing to the opposition of some important sectors of public opinion, particularly in this continent—not only in the United States. But Article XI is the most important Article of the Covenant. It is the core of the Covenant. As I have to come back to it on another account, more important than this one, I shall not justify my statement now. But this article, which is the very heart of the Covenant, has been rendered nugatory, particularly in the all-important case of Manchuria, because of a misapplication—a rigid and, to my mind, an absurd application of the unanimity rule. Under Article XI, the Council must take any action that may be deemed wise and effectual to safeguard the peace of nations. It is evident that in such activities the Council must, if necessary, act without the acquiescence of the interested parties, or of one of them if it "deems it wise and effectual." But on the plea that Article XI is an article of conciliation, the rule of unanimity was rigidly applied, even to matters of mere expediency.

Article VIII in its Paragraph 2 also safeguards the unlimited sovereignty of states; because in its Paragraph 1, Article VIII prescribes there must be a reduction of armaments to the minimum amount compatible with national safety and the maintenance of international obligations, while in Paragraph 2 it prescribes that the Council shall prepare plans for disarmament and *submit* them to the governments concerned. It is for the governments to *decide* whether they will disarm or not, and their sovereignty remains unimpaired.

Again Article XII prescribes that no war can take place during the three months that follow the decision taken by an Arbitral Commission, the Council, or the World Court, on any particular conflict; but says nothing about what may happen after those three months. Now this ominous silence is best explained by what happened before a justice of the peace in a small village in Spain, where a priest had knocked down a man who had slapped him in the face. The justice of the peace asked the priest if he was not aware of the fact that it is said in the gospels that when we are smitten on the right cheek, we must offer our left. And the priest answered, "Yes, I am aware of it. He smote me on the right and I did offer my left, but our Lord does not say what you must do afterward."

There are two important reservations of sovereignty in Article XV, Paragraphs 7 and 8. The first of these concerns the case when, a conflict having been put before the Council, there is no unanimity, and in that case the Article says that the states concerned reserve to themselves the right to take such action as they shall consider necessary for the maintenance of right and justice. It means they can do as they please.

And in Paragraph 8 there is an exception of domestic jurisdiction which is due to the insistence of the delegation of the United States when the Covenant was drafted. If a case is recognized as one which international law reserves for the internal jurisdiction of a country, then the Council shall so report and shall make no recommendation as to its settlement.

Finally, there is still a trace of unlimited sovereignty in the second paragraph of Article XVI, which is the paragraph on what is called sanctions. The Council may *recommend*—but no more than *recommend*—the armed forces which any one nation may be called upon to contribute to maintaining the law of the Covenant against a transgressor state.

The number of places in the Covenant in which the sovereignty of states remains unimpaired is therefore considerable. They are witnesses of the strength of the principle of sovereignty, even in that relatively wonderful atmosphere in which the Covenant was drafted.

## Sovereignty Limited by the Covenant
### Judicial Limitations

Let us now pass to the cases in which sovereignty is limited. Of course from the legal point of view, the whole Covenant is an instrument for the limitation of sovereignty; but it is important to point out that the juridical—and merely juridical—limitation of sovereignty has no more power in it than that which the other social and moral forces in the community in question put behind the respect of the law. A law is only efficient when it has become life. We might even say that a law is only efficient when it is life made into law. A law once in this country attempted in vain to regulate the liquid nourishment of its citizens. It was never really effective; at least not in the sense in which it was meant to be. Why? Because it was too far removed from the habits of the country. Similarly, in the Covenant, if the Covenant were only a legal instrument and there were no other forces, no other social collective moral forces to strengthen and give life to this legal aspect of the Covenant there would not be much in it of limitation of sovereignty, even though from the strictly verbal, formal, and juridical point of view it is a considerable, in fact unprecedented, instrument for the limitation of sovereignty.

Organic Limitations
A. Limitation by Solidarity

We shall then have to deal successively with several of these forces which in reality operate through the forms of the juridical limitation, and first of all with a series of them, no less than five, which come under the common aspect of what we might call *organic* forces, that is to say, all those forces which spring from the fact that the world community is already an established organism. The first of them flows from a principle which we have already discussed—the principle of solidarity. Under solidarity we find in the Covenant no less than four articles. Two of them are really beautiful and the other two are, I believe, possibly mistaken.

The two splendid articles in the Covenant are Articles X and XI. Article X we have read a minute ago when discussing the question of unanimity. It establishes the principle of solidarity whenever an aggression is made against the territorial integrity or the political independence of any one of the members of the League; for it implies that this violation of a principle offends all the members of the community who see themselves threatened in the threat which afflicts their neighbors.

It is a well-known fact that, for political reasons of considerable importance, mainly due to the fact that the Covenant was born in an atmosphere of war and may be suspected, not perhaps altogether unfairly, of contributing to crystallizing the results of that war, Article X has been the object of a considerable amount of opposition. But no reproach whatsoever can be addressed to Article XI. It is the core of the Covenant, and it is admirably drafted. It seems to be the only article in the Covenant which is en-

tirely due, personally, to President Wilson. More honor
to his memory.

Any war or threat of war, whether immediately affecting any
of the members of the League or not, is hereby declared a matter
of concern to the whole League; and the League shall take any
action that may be deemed wise and effectual to safeguard the
peace of Nations.

In case any such emergency should arise, the Secretary General shall, on the request of any member of the League, forth-
with summon a meeting of the Council.

It is also declared to be the friendly right of each member
of the League to bring to the attention of the Assembly or of
the Council any circumstances whatever affecting international
relations which threaten to disturb international peace or the
good of the understanding between nations upon which peace
depends.

Two principles are here established. The first is that
any war or threat of war is a matter of concern to the
League; that is to say, the principle of the existence of a
community of states is strongly emphasized and the first
paragraph implies, therefore, that any war pressure exerted
on any part of that body and soul called the League is felt
by the whole League, which is the principle of all organisms. An organism is a congeries of cells in which the sensi-
bility is unified, and wherever the pain is inflicted the
organism in its entirety feels the pain and takes the decision. It is therefore the most concrete assertion of the
organic nature of the League to be found in the Covenant.

The second principle is that any one of the members of
the League has the right to draw attention to any such situation, of threat to the whole in any of its parts. In the old
days if any one nation A called attention to any situation
arising between two other nations, B and C, that nation

A would probably have been the object of an energetic "Mind your own business." Now this second paragraph of Article XI establishes, as it was indispensable to do in international law, because the principle did not exist before—in fact, the reverse principle very definitely existed—that any one nation *has* the right to call the attention of the League to any situation, however distant from its shores, which, according to that nation, threatens international peace or the good understanding on which the peace of nations rests. And if a nation takes such action no one, and particularly none of the nations directly concerned, can take umbrage at it, because there it is, written in the Covenant!

Curiously enough, this second paragraph is one of those which illustrate the point mentioned above, that the law must not run too far ahead of life because in spite of it there is no question that if a nation invokes it whose immediate and direct interest in the matter in question is not evident, it is absolutely certain that the effect would be disconcerting in the international community and that people would start asking, "What is behind it all?"

So possibly this second paragraph may be a little ahead not certainly of *things,* but at any rate of mental habits, mental and political habits. Which, in its turn, is not so much a pessimistic as an optimistic observation because, while this second paragraph, which demands less important action than the first, would in its application at the hands of any one nation be considered perhaps as a little unusual and odd on the part of the more directly interested countries, the first paragraph which calls in, not any one nation but the whole League, is swallowed absolutely and entirely by everybody; which shows that the idea of the world community has made so much progress in the world that energetic action from the whole of the League is more acceptable than action even less important, even more moderate, on the part of any member thereof.

Articles XVI and XVII, particularly in the third paragraph of the letter, are also to be mentioned under the heading of solidarity. They are, perhaps, less well inspired than Articles X and XI. For Article XVI is an article entirely based on punishment, and the idea of punishment in the world community is not in its place. The world community is not so very much bigger than any one of its members, to be able to carry on punishment efficiently; and in any case punishment amongst the nations can only take the form of war, or of actions so unfriendly that they are bound to lead to a spirit of war and possibly to actions of war. Now war amongst states, whatever its cause, sooner or later is bound to take the shape that the laws of war demand, and not the laws of peace.

So that this Article, though based on a healthy spirit of solidarity as to its *aims,* owing to the *means* which this solidarity seeks to express itself in, takes on an anti-solidarity point of view which makes of it a contradiction within itself.

Similar observations apply to Article XVII, Paragraph 3, which is merely an extension of Article XVI, to the case in which the transgressor state happens to be a nation outside the Covenant.

## B. Limitations by Public Opinion

The second force of an organic nature acting through the Covenant in limitation of sovereignty is public opinion. And this covers the cases in the Covenant in which the appeal is made to public opinion. We shall have to come later to cases arising directly from the play of these forces in inter-

national life; but it is already interesting to find, in this in-
ventory of the causes of world union that limit sovereignty
*within* the Covenant, this most important cause of limitation of sovereignty which is public opinion. The draftsmen
of the Covenant realized it and appealed to public opinion
relatively frequently.

For instance, Article XIV sets up the World Court. And
in setting up the World Court it already lays down a pro-
cedure developed in the World Court statute and known
as *Advisory Opinion*. If the Council so desires, instead of
taking a matter legally before the Court for a decision, it
merely asks the Court to give an advisory opinion. An advisory opinion of the Court has no legal value. It is merely
published; the Council can use it in its argument for
negotiating the case, and that is the end of it. Nevertheless, it is one of the most powerful weapons in the armory of
the institutions for peace, for it is evident that when the
World Court has given an advisory opinion on a question,
its moral power is just short of that which a sentence would
have. This has been so felt by the opponents of the World
Court in this country, who have made it a condition for
the entrance of America into the World Court that the
Council should not ask for advisory opinions on matters
interesting this country, without the vote of this country.

In the Council of the League of Nations this tendency
manifested in the United States is obvious in many of the
important nations, and we of the Spanish delegation often
had to announce to the Council that if the matter was not
put on a better footing we would ask for a regular discussion as to whether the Council can ask an advisory opinion,
without having to vote unanimously on it. Many of the
nations of the League, including Soviet Russia, I am sorry
to say—for no one can be on the left all the time and on

every subject—claimed that the votes would have to be unanimous; we were of the opinion that it should be by a simple majority vote.

Article XV, Paragraph 4, also appeals to public opinion, as well as Paragraph 5. They are the articles which describe what happens when the Council takes up a question, or a conflict, and decides it. The Council publishes its report. If there is no unanimity the Council can do no more; but it publishes the report and leaves it at the door of public opinion, and if any of the members of the Council disagree, they are at liberty—in fact, they are so advised by the Covenant—to declare their own opinion; so that in the end the question is put before the court of public opinion. Let us incidentally observe that in the Covenant in all appeals to public opinion, the opinion in question is that of the world, not that of any one nation.

A similar remark applies to the tenth paragraph of Article XV. This paragraph prescribes that if, and in certain conditions, one of the parties so desires, a conflict which has been before the Council under Article XV must pass on to the Assembly. As a matter of fact, that always means that if a question has not been solved in the quiet atmosphere of private negotiations behind the doors of the Council, it is thrown open to the public in the Assembly.

This is again a clear appeal to public opinion, as is also Article XVIII, which prescribes that no treaty is valid between any two or more nations that has not been registered with the Secretariat of the League of Nations and published by it. The aim of this publication of treaties is automatically to denounce these treaties that do not adjust to the precepts of the Covenant and, in general, to the international morality of our day.

A similar appeal to public opinion is made in Paragraph 7 of Article XXII, this being the article that institutes the system of mandates for colonial territories, and its Paragraph 7 prescribing that a report on what has happened in the mandated territories in the year must be published by the Council.

### C. Limitations Under the Permanent Mandate of the League

There is yet a third consideration which illustrates the organic character of the League and of the limitations to the Covenant which it implies—namely the permanent character of the duty laid on the League and its organizations for the carrying on of the affairs of the world. There are a number of permanent duties which are performed by the League. Curiously enough, the whole thing starts with a general, permanent duty, defined in Article III, Paragraph 3, and Article IV, Paragraph 4, as well as in Article III, Paragraph 2, and Article IV, Paragraph 3. We had better read these texts to make it quite clear that we are in the presence of permanent institutions with a general, permanent mandate.

Says Paragraph 3 of Article III: "The Assembly may deal at its meetings with any matter within the sphere of action of the League or affecting the peace of the world."

Paragraph 4 of Article IV extends the same principle to the Council: "The Council may deal at its meetings with any matter within the sphere of action of the League or affecting the peace of the world."

And, lest this general mandate were evaded by not meeting, Paragraph 2 of Article III on the Assembly, and Paragraph 3 of Article IV on the Council, say: "The Assembly shall meet at stated intervals and from time to time, as occasion may require, at the seat of the League or at such other place as may be decided upon."

"The Council shall meet from time to time as occasion may require and at least once a year at the seat of the League or at such other place as may be decided upon."

In the beginning, therefore, it was thought that the Council could do with one sitting a year. It never has had less than three, and there have been years when it had seven, eight, nine, or ten. As for the Assembly, the Covenant does not say how many times it should meet. It merely speaks of "stated intervals." It has always had a minimum of one meeting a year, and some years has met two or even more times. This shows that the permanent mandate entrusted to the League Council and Assembly by the draftsmen of the Covenant has been fulfilled and that its activities have gone beyond that which the most enthusiastic creators of the League at the time imagined.

Article IV creates the Secretariat, and there again we meet with a permanent institution. Let me say in passing that if the League had done nothing more than creating an international civil service such as the Secretariat of the League and of the Labor Office, with so much devotion, intelligence, and impartiality in the management of international affairs, it would have been justified!

We have yet more articles of this type, showing the spirit and tendency of the drafters of the Covenant. Paragraphs 4 and 5 of Article VII prescribe that the members of the Secretariat of the League shall have diplomatic immunity and inviolatibility, just like the diplomatic representative of any nation on the territory of any other nation. Article XIV, creating the World Court, also puts forward an obviously permanent world institution.

Article XVII, watching over what nations that are not members of the League of Nations do, is a curious example of the kind of world care which was the inspiration of the drafters of the Covenant.

Article XVIII, a guarantee that treaties are in harmony with the Covenant, again lays a permanent obligation on the League. Article XIX, which is the article that provides that treaties which are no longer applicable may be revised by the League of Nations, is again of a permanent and general character; and so are Articles XXII, XXIII, and XXIV—Article XXII on mandates and XXIII on several social duties, such as the protection of women and children and the question of traffic in arms; and Article XXIV providing that all international offices will gradually fall under the sway of the League of Nations. It is therefore evident that the idea that the League is a permanent institution with some permanent duties, both in a general sense and in a specific sense, is represented in the Covenant by a very high number of articles.

### D. Limitations Through the Executive and Legislative Powers of the League

Finally, there are two further aspects of this organic character of the League of Nations, in the executive functions and the legislative functions which are given to the Council and to the Assembly by the Covenant.

The executive function is given to the Council under Article VIII about disarmament, and under Articles X, XI, and XVI in matters of aggression and security. We have already discussed them. Here they are merely recalled as examples of legislative authority granted by the Covenant, and therefore by the nations whose sovereignty is melted into the Covenant, to the Council and to the Assembly.

And the legislative authority is granted in Article VIII, Paragraph 4, where it is said that after a plan for disarmament has been approved, no nation can alter its own armaments without consulting the Covenant of the League of Nations—a clear legislative function given to the Council, if only of a negative character.

It might perhaps be good to add here, though this does not come strictly under Covenant description, but merely as a matter of parallel, that the International Labor Office, based on part 13 of the Treaty of Versailles, ratified separately from the Treaty by many nations, including America, belonging to the organization of labor, grants to the Labor Conference higher legislative powers even than those granted to the Assembly and the Council, since the conventions that have been drafted and approved by the Labor Conferences are bound to be put before their respective parliaments, without the objection of the executives at home being sufficient to paralyze the power of the International Labor Conference in this respect.

## Ethical Limitations

Having discussed the legal and organic aspects of the Covenant, we come now to one which is perhaps the most interesting of all and ultimately the one on which the force of the whole rests—what we might call the ethical aspect of the Covenant. It is apparent in the Preamble, in which the aims of the Covenant are established in a clear fashion, as preëminently moral; and appears also in Article VIII, Paragraph 6, and in Article XVI, Paragraph 4. Let us read first the preamble:

The high contracting parties, in order to promote international coöperation and to achieve international peace and security, by the acceptance of obligations not to resort to war,

by the prescription of open, just, and honorable relations between nations,

by the firm establishment of the understandings of international law as the actual rule of conduct among governments, and

by the maintenance of international justice and scrupulous respect for all treaty obligations in the dealings of the organized peoples with one another,

agree to this Covenant of the League of Nations.

The ethical character of this treaty is evident. It appears also, in Paragraph 6 of Article VIII, because this paragraph is one of the most advanced stipulations in the Covenant, since it touches upon one of the most delicate aspects of international life, that of armaments, which is generally defined or described prudishly as "national defense":

The members of the League undertake to interchange full and frank information as to the scale of their armaments, their military, naval, and air programs and the condition of such of their industries as are adaptable to warlike purposes.

It will be seen that this is a far, far cry and a far, far advance on the system of spies; but the system of spies continues.

This is what I have to say on the Covenant as an instrument for the limitation of sovereignty amongst nations.

### Limitations of Sovereignty Outside the Covenant
### Financial and Economic

We are to discuss now other sets of limitations of sovereignty which obtain in international life and without which our picture would be evidently incomplete.

First, the financial and economic limitations to sovereignty. The financial limitation is generally known as the "hidden hand." The hidden hand of the financier is one of the well-known pictures in the imaginations of political writers. There is a good deal of romance about this, although in reality it has some substance. Those who are particularly interested in the subject would do well to ponder over a most able work on the matter, written by Eugene Staley, of the University of Chicago, on *War and the Private Investor*. The facts seem to be that we cannot say that the financier pushes the state, his state, to back his interest in other nations, any more than that the state pushes the financier to occupy with his finance the particular nation that the statesman has his eye on at the time.

The balance would probably be that the two forces act together, that in the back of the two actions is a certain tendency of a particular nation, with force all around, to expand and increase its power, and that now the state will push the financier, now the financier will push the state. Without in any way claiming that there are no exceptions, one might say that the network of international finance tends to break down when a strong nationalistic interest demands it.

There are, nevertheless, cases in which economic considerations take a very important part in the shaping of the foreign policy of nations. If a nation is relatively small compared to another, and that other nation absorbs a considerable portion of its foreign trade, it cannot be said that the first nation has an unimpaired sovereignty; the economic tie is too important; the economic consequences of the abuse of sovereignty on the part of the bigger state by punishing the small power, on the score of economic consumption, are too great, and therefore this is a clear case in which sovereignty is limited by economic considerations. There are cases even in which that sovereignty practically

vanishes. There are countries which are practically owned
by a particular firm of foreign bankers. The sovereignty in
this sort of case almost vanishes.

## Moral Pride

But as the world progresses, that ethical force which we
saw active in connection with the Covenant comes to the
fore. The progress in ethical standards extends to this
sphere of international relations. Pride is a curious moral
phenomenon, and moral pride is one of the most interesting aspects of it. Moral pride is a source of power, for
through moral pride we raise our standard and force ourselves to do what, without moral pride, we should be too
indolent to perform; but moral pride sometimes, in the
international sphere, becomes a source of impotence, because we do not want to risk the condemnation of public
opinion by putting before the whole world the turpitude
of our intentions. There are actions which, in the international sphere, were committed by the free and immoral
nations of the Western World, no more than about twenty-
five or thirty years ago which they would not be able to
commit today, because their own public opinion would
not allow it! It may be sinning on the side of optimism, but
it does not seem that a behavior such as that of Italy in
Abyssinia would have been possible on the part of any one
of the governments of the democratically governed countries.

From a certain point of view, therefore, it looks as if
ethics, the growth of ethics, should be propping up the
sovereignty of the weaker states, and therefore we might
find ourselves in the somewhat paradoxical situation that a
progress in ethics would be stimulating an international
force in which we are not particularly interested—sover-

eignty; but here again the balance is on the good side, because here sovereignty is not threatened as sovereignty in general but only as sovereignty in the case of big states, and only at the hands of sovereignty in the case of big states, very powerful states. Moreover, the sovereignty of the small states is not thereby protected by any internal national force but on the contrary by the action of a universal force of ethics, which grows and rises in public opinion, in the *world* public opinion. So it comes to this, that more and more sovereignties, high and low, tend to be equalized on being rooted in the ethical opinion of the world.

# IV

# THE NON-NATIONAL PATTERN

WE have been dealing so far with a pattern of world affairs which was, as the very word says, *international,* i. e., inter-*national,* that is to say, national. We have been observing forces which, acting in the world field, were nevertheless national as to shape and origin and acted through nations or groups of nations.

We are now to discuss all that which in world affairs does not follow the national pattern, all that which butts into sovereignty, sideways, or from above, or from below.

As with all that precedes, we do not propose, by any means, to analyze fully every one of the aspects of world life with which I deal; we have neither time nor competence for that, for world life is a vast ocean of facts, emotions, ideals, traditions, which no man can chart and fathom. All we mean to do is to enumerate and allude to the forces acting in world life which do not adjust to the national pattern, and put them, so far as possible, each in its place in the general picture.

## WORLD BUSINESS

The first non-national pattern which occurs to the mind is what we might call the business pattern. There are in life, in contemporary life, a number of activities in the field of business which do not follow the national pattern. A typical example is oil. The arms of some of the great businesses that deal in oil might well be a wide-winged eagle with the motto "Oil spreads." Oil is one of the most powerful elements in international life. It has a tremendous importance as the source of motive power for navies and for aircraft. And therefore the control of oil has become one of the important, indeed essential, elements in what is prudishly called "national defense."

Another of these types of business that do not follow the national pattern is cables, connected to the national pattern through the moral influence of news. Another is the automobile industry, also connected to the national pattern through the growing importance of motorization in armies and its connection with aircraft. In fact it would be vain to try to exhaust the list of all these businesses that, owing to the inherent vitality in them, have gone far beyond the size of any one nation and have become extremely complicated, not merely from the point of view of the territory in which the business is installed, but from the point of view of the actual power behind and of the real men that are in control. In most cases this kind of business, as is the case with finance, may be at times an instrument of sovereignty, at times a promoter or at least a factor in this direction which is given to sovereignty in international affairs.

Rubber is a case in point. It is well known that on the occasion of some readjustments of the price of rubber in the world, there was a considerable dissatisfaction of a political character between this country and Great Britain to the extent that many people thought, and even tried to prove with figures—and I do not take sides—that Great Britain got back whatever she gave to this country as a war debt by increasing the price of rubber. Now rubber is not controlled by the Government of England; nevertheless, it would be difficult to say that rubber is not controlled by certain agencies with influence over the British Government or in close touch with the British Government; so that in the last resort the direction of the currents of power which brought about that decision on the price of rubber would remain the secret of one or two individual brains.

What happens with this world tissue, this world pattern of important raw materials and finance? Generally it does not break but it yields; it yields without breaking, and the relations that are not strictly national in this kind of world business are strained, apparently even are broken; but in reality resist, and in most cases the tissue is not altogether destroyed.

The fact remains that we have here one of the most important elements of world life which does not follow the national pattern, one which impinges on sovereignty in ways which may sometimes be positive, sometimes negative, which may sometimes help sovereignty, sometimes hinder its full use and, in any case, complicate the apparently simple pattern of sixty absolutely separate powers combining or not combining, coöperating or not coöperating. Above, below, aside from the sixty, or sixty-three powers, that seem as if they were completely independent, we are going to find a growing number of world activities, of world forms of life which do not follow the national pattern and which, therefore, in one way or another, constitute teguments, tissues, adhesions, that prevent these sixty separate sovereignties from behaving in a completely free way.

### RELIGION

It is a far cry from business to religion, but it is probably fair to say that after business, the most powerful element in world life that does not follow the national pattern is religion.

The Christian religions differ considerably in that there

is one of them which must be separated from all the others as to its power for cohesion and coördination of effort. The Roman Catholic faith, by the length and continuity of its tradition, by the fact that it is an international authority and though today practically, though not altogether, devoid of territory, is generally recognized as a power, as a spiritual power, yet a power with diplomatic representation and a certain number of the privileges and forms of nationality or sovereignty. This fact, combined with the stronger discipline with which local and national units are held by the Vatican and greater unification of dogma and practice, makes of the Catholic religion one of the most important, and certainly the most important in the religious field, of the elements of non-national pattern in the world.

We have nevertheless been able to observe in recent times, such as for instance in the World War, that in spite of the theoretical universality of the Roman Catholic religion, and of the theoretical universal brotherhood of its dogma, the Roman Catholic religion has been unable to maintain an impartiality on a line above the struggle, as we might have thought that it would do, at least in modern times. Not only has this been observable in the extremely difficult cases presented to it by the World War, but in a more regrettable way, we have observed it with regard to the Abyssinian question, in which possibly it may have been that the Roman Catholic Church has shown itself more Roman than Catholic.

The Protestant variety of the Christian religion, owing to the extraordinary multiplicity of its forms of worship and discipline, is a much less important element in the extra-national pattern than the Roman Catholic religion. And though in the fields of pacifism it has maintained a much

more courageous and a stronger line than the Roman
Catholic faith, the very fact of this multiplicity has acted
against its strength as a world factor. It may nevertheless
be argued plausibly that the Protestant faiths have not
always been above acting as instruments of national and
even of nationalistic penetration. Missions are not always
exclusively religious. Culture provides an easy bridge between the universal of religion and the local of nationality
or even of nationalism. In this respect, we must consider
the Christian citizens as world forces, inherently of a universal character, practically at times within the national
pattern. Nor is this altogether untrue either in what concerns the Roman Catholic faith.

The Jewish faith is a strong world factor of a non-
national pattern, but the Jewish faith is mostly strong in
world affairs owing to a special characteristic of it, namely,
the fact that it rests also on a racial factor—the Jewish race,
an extremely important element for the leavening of world
unification. At the moment, when it is reviled and perse-
cuted in some nations, it is perhaps worth remembering
that the world owes to the Jews a great debt of civilization,
for they have been, in all epochs of history, the providers
of great men, of great philosophers, of great doctors, great
scientists, even to the present date and even, of late, statesmen. Many of the objections raised against the Jewish race
are in reality created by the centuries-long Christian perse-
cution of them, which has determined some of their racial
characteristics.

In this review of world factors, this peculiar race without a territory, leavening all the nations of the world, creating amongst them a system of communication of ideas and
trade, of commerce, both intellectual and material, is un-

doubtedly one of the most important factors of world life and one which, precisely because it does not follow the national pattern, is of the utmost importance for a system of unification. For the Jew has a wonderful capacity for becoming a national of any one nation and yet remaining in touch with the Jews of other nations; an excellent system for national inter-communication in itself, and while it may be badly used—everything in the world may be badly used—the fact remains that they may be, and they often are, most useful elements of international communication and understanding. Moreover, it is an indubitable fact that in world life the number of idealistic Jews is considerable.

Islam is also an international religion. Islam always was an exceptionally interesting religion in that it always was free from nationalism. In fact, Islam is in itself a kind of nation; it is not unlike the Jewish religion, in that it is a kind of nation without a territory, even though it often possessed many territories. We should go out of the boundaries of our work here if we tried to specialize, or even entered into a description of the revival of Islam which is at present taking place, but it seems not doubtful that in our present era we shall have to count on the contribution which Islam may bring to world affairs as a religion, devoid of the poison of nationalism.

Far Eastern religions are also, naturally, elements of international life out of the national pattern but, except for the national religion of Japan, the religions of the East are the least political of religions. They are the most other-worldly and therefore probably will be the least influential in the strictly political life of the world. Nevertheless, for what they are, they will have to be counted amongst these elements of non-national pattern which we are at present describing.

## MARXISM

After the religious patterns, we must consider one which is very similar in emotional aspect to religion: the Marxist pattern, also a typically world pattern, or at any rate a typically non-national pattern of world life. It is rationalistic in form, emotional and possibly even religious in content. Its internationalism dates from the very beginning. From the very first times of the Manifesto of Marx and Engels, the international aspect of Marxism has been put forward as its most important element. "Workers of the world, unite!" has been from the very first its cry; therefore it is eminently one of the forces with which we must count in a review of world life. Its real international import is only beginning to assert itself now, possibly, under Communism, for all of us except the youngest perhaps remember how shocked the world was when in 1914 all the promises of international help that the workers had made to each other across the frontiers broke down at the first sounds of the clarion call. All the same, there is a new note, a new ring in Marxism, in contemporary days, and undoubtedly amongst the forces that are cutting across sovereignty and aiming toward the establishment of a united world, Marxism is one of the most important. And it is here time to record that the Union of Socialistic Soviet Republics is, in its very name, a world union, open to any republic that may be formed in the future on its pattern. If Marxism freed itself from the great error of class war which it carries within itself, it certainly would be the most potent force for world unification in our epoch.

## ANTI-MARXISM OR FASCISM

It is difficult to refer to the Marxist pattern without bringing to mind the anti-Marxist pattern, or Fascist-Nazi pattern, which appeared of late on our world horizon. It is a paradox that a political school based on the emphasizing of nationalism should claim an international import, and that it should try to make proselytes and to engage in alliances on the basis of similar régime. It is a paradox because internationalism cannot be based on the exaggeration and assertion of nationalism. And of course these alliances on the basis of régime do not work; if the nations that are, may we say, afflicted with these systems try to unite on the basis that their systems are similar, namely that they both wear a colored shirt, they soon find that the colors don't go together; because one of them seeks, not opposite aims from the other but the same aims, that is to say, they both want to eat the same cake, which always develops enmity—even among Fascists.

### THE CONTINENTAL PATTERN

We come now to a pattern of a non-national character but one which presents, in our contemporary history, a considerable importance—the continental pattern. From the contemporary intellectual point of view, it arises out of the feeling that possibly we may have been too ambitious in trying to erect a world construction straightway, instead of applying our efforts first to more modest tasks and organizing first our continents, uniting them later into a higher structure. But this is what we might call *a posteriori* rationalization. As a matter of fact, the continental tendency appears in history far back in different periods of the history of the continents—certainly as far back as the fifteenth century in Europe, and as far back as President Monroe in the Continent of America.

The European type of mind is already discernible in Charles V, and in Napoleon, before we come to Briand.

Charles V saw the union of Europe on a religious basis, and there is a most fascinating speech addressed by him in 1530 to the Pope in Bologna in which, after having accused Francis I of all kinds of misdemeanors, including an alliance with the Grand Turk, he put forward his view that nothing could be done in the way of peace except by making a unit of Europe. He may be considered as the first man with a European outlook. He was beaten because he came too soon, because he came just at the time when Europe was to undergo its deepest division, owing to the religious wars.

It may be interesting to note how it is precisely at the moment when Europe is rent by its deepest mental divisions that the great Europeans think of uniting it; because Briand, the statesman, with Coudenhove-Kalergi, the intellectual, behind him, thought of establishing the United States of Europe at the moment when Europe was on the eve of another religious war, the war between Fascism and Communism, which is now more or less theoretically, and sometimes practically, afflicting it.

Napoleon himself—not perhaps the Napoleon who triumphed at Austerlitz, but the Napoleon already under the shadow of death—thought of the Union of Europe and of establishing all over Europe one only system of law courts preliminary to one only system of economic and political life.

In America, the unification of the continent begins both on the Spanish-American side and on the Anglo-Saxon-American side quite early in the century. Bolivar, in his congress at Panama, thought already of unifying all the republics of Spanish America, and the Monroe Doctrine was already in itself a kind of assertion of the unity of this country, at any rate from the point of view of its political relationship to other continents. The Monroe Doctrine, in its evolution, has become more and more an element of unification, but not always in a direct way, since it passed through times when it threatened to be an element of division between the two Americas, the Spanish and the Anglo-Saxon America, owing to the excessive unilateral character which it took under some of your presidents and particularly under Roosevelt the First; it has been considerably rejuvenated under Roosevelt the Second.

It is interesting to note that the Monroe Doctrine has been imitated by Japan in Asia. Possibly not under its best aspects; perhaps Japan, being a little behind the times in its evolution, is still at the epoch of Roosevelt the First, and has still to find out its policy under a Japanese Roosevelt the Second who may come later—let us hope not too late.

Now what is to be thought, what should we think, about this continental pattern? To begin with, there is no question but that it offers to the mind a kind of rest between the idea of the nation and the idea of a world union, and from that point of view it is a useful stage in the education of the mind in its effort to rise from the nation, meeting higher responsibilities. It is the first step toward a union; but only if it means to be so—only if it is not a step toward exclusion; if the continental idea means the establishment round a continent of a kind of fence for the exclusion of other than continental life, we can hardly consider that as a progress in world affairs. It is a progress in world affairs if the continent is considered as a step toward world synthesis. But this question of the value of continents in world affairs had better be left for further analysis at a later stage in our discussion.

### INTERNATIONAL COÖPERATION

Let us now take on another aspect of the non-national pattern in world affairs, namely, the pattern of international coöperation. There are three kinds of international coöperation already afoot.[1] There is first the growing number of *official* institutions, what we might call the institutions of the world state, or *toward* the world state. They are the League of Nations, the International Labor Office, the Institute of Agriculture at Rome, the International Institute of Private Law at Rome, the International Institute of Cinematograph for Education at Rome, and the Institute of Intellectual Coöperation at Paris. There may be others which I forget, of what you might call the solar system of the League, than those that I have enumerated, and there is one outside the League but strictly official, and possibly the only world-state institution there is: I refer to the Postal Union at Bern.

The growth of these institutions, all of which, except the Postal Union, date from 1920 onwards, shows with what a tremendous vitality the yearning for a world state has become manifest in the twentieth century immediately after the World War. This yearning for the world state was already manifest before the War, in pre-war institution of a *semi-official* character, such as the Interparliamentary Union, an association of members of parliament of the free parliamentary countries, with a permanent secretariat and a yearly conference for dealing with world affairs. There is an institution of a similar kind, of a semi-official character,

[1] See on this subject the admirable treatise written by Dr. Christian Lange, who was for a long time Secretary-General of the Interparliamentary Union in Geneva.

created since the War which has been taking a growing importance in not, unfortunately, the management of the affairs of the world but at any rate the study of the affairs of the world, the International Chamber of Commerce.

Finally, there is a third category: the *purely private* category, composed of an immense number of world associations or international associations of all kinds and aims built on a non-national pattern.

There are at least five categories here that are important: the business, the religious, the political, the scientific, and the sporting association, all very important for the development of the feeling of mutual understanding and the growth of that feeling of the international tegument or tissue which binds nations together in an organic whole.

This may be the place to point out how much mischief is being done in the world by the exploitation of nationalistic emotions in international sporting events such as football matches and others. These events create bitterness similar to that of war and should be checked by international authorities.

### COMPETITION; COÖPERATION; ORGANIC LIFE

All these efforts point to an evolution of world affairs; perhaps even more to an evolution of our way of understanding world affairs which, starting from the competitive point of view, goes through the coöperative point of view, and is bound to end in the organic point of view. If we consider what international life was, say one hundred years ago, to make this point much clearer, we discover that then world life, the relations between the nations of the world, were based on a competitive philosophy. The world of nations was far behind the world of individuals. The nations considered their sovereignty absolutely unlimited

by any law as no man or woman would ever consider his
liberty unlimited, for the immense majority of men and
women of the civilized countries, badly as they might
sometimes behave, at any rate more or less roughly followed a moral law and kept to a moral law and there was a
considerable number of things which they might have
done, yet would not do. The majority of people, for instance, were not murderers or thieves one hundred years
ago.

The majority of the nations, however, were both murderers and thieves. There was absolutely no moral law that
prevented a nation, one hundred years ago, from destroy-
ing another nation, from robbing it, from murdering its
nationals and from behaving in an almost cannibalistic
manner. The lag between the collective human being
called Nation, and the individual human being, which was
the national, was measurable in centuries of moral development and evolution. That was the time in which world
life could be defined as strictly competitive.

Gradually there developed the coöperative point of
view. Doubtless it always existed up to a point, even in
the days of competitive policy. All the human tendencies
exist at practically all the moments of history, and the co-
operative point of view did not just appear out of the blue
*after* the competitive point of view. This point of view was
present in such a tiny proportion as to account for practically nothing in world affairs until there began to grow
that sense of *objective solidarity* which we discussed in our
first lecture, and which, willy nilly, forced human beings,
even human beings who have to carry on the painful government of countries, to realize that a certain minimum
of coöperation is indispensable, even in international politics.

Right through the nineteenth century, along with the maintaining at a very high pitch of the urge and tension of competition between nations, there develops, nevertheless, owing to the pressure of financial, economic, and mental communications, a certain sense of coöperation between nations. This is the period which sees the wonderful growth of world associations, and also the formation of the first official interstate or international institution in the Postal Union.

Then begin also certain more or less inter-financial or international organizations for concrete aims, such as the Suez Canal, commissions for the administration of certain international rivers or straits, and similar forms of co-operative life. It is a movement that began, perhaps, in the Congress of Vienna—a congress that was by no means as reactionary in international affairs as the names of some of its eminent members for national affairs might suggest; and it gained a good deal of impetus through the growth of international practical coöperation, which was taking place in other than political fields.

But the coöperative sense of international affairs finds its maximum with the Covenant of the League of Nations, in which the words "coöperation," "coöperation in international affairs," actually are written in the first paragraph of the Preamble. It is then a political outlook—what you might call a subconscious political philosophy, which sees these sixty nations, as sixty partners or sixty human beings who choose to collaborate, as they might choose not to collaborate, who have the freedom to decide whether they are going to collaborate or whether they are not going to collaborate.

That is the maximum stage at which the thought of the most advanced of us had reached at the moment when the

Covenant of the League of Nations was written. The war had given to all those people who in Paris were drafting the Treaty, and therefore the Covenant, which is its first part, a very keen idea of the necessity of coöperating because, under the strong influence of objective solidarity due to the feeling of common danger, the allied and associated nations had been driven to constitute a series of coöperating organizations, riding over frontiers in order to administer their resources, which were strained to the breaking point by the vitality and the ruthless methods of the enemy. The characteristic type of these institutions created by the war was the Allied Shipping Control Board, which was put in the hands of Sir Arthur Salter. But when the war was over, these magnificent institutions of world coöperation were very quickly lost—thrown into the fire— as if they had been dangerous elements in the progress of the world, because there were two or three powerful enemies of these forms of life, and not all of them were inspired in sovereignty.

These institutions disappeared, but the lesson that had inspired them had not disappeared and was incorporated in the Covenant. Yet even these lessons and even this Covenant were not fully cognizant of the extent to which the institutions created had gone beyond the mere conception of coöperation.

It is no longer coöperation that is going to save civilization from the disaster of international anarchy. If we are going to take to heart the lesson of the war, and still more so the lessons of the post-war, we must go one step forward, and that step forward is that which separates the coöperative conception of international affairs from the organic conception of world affairs. The nations of the world are not merely like sixty individuals, standing and moving sep-

arately and in an interrelated way, that may choose to co-
operate or may choose not to coöperate; the nations of the
world are organically united in such a way that they have
become members of each other and members of a higher
organization which is mankind, at present, unfortunately,
disorganized but not inorganic. Mankind is disorganized
but is not inorganic; it is one because all the movements
in life, in mankind, whether they are material or moral or
mental, circulate freely through mankind independently of
frontiers. Even in the presence of the obstacles put before
them by censorships in one case or by customs in the other
case, the fact remains that the elements of mental and material life circulate through all mankind. All that customs
can do is to throttle, up to a point, the flow of goods and of
finance through the frontiers; and all that censorship can
do is to refract the rays of knowledge, the rays of light that
pass from one environment to another when a frontier is
crossed, but not altogether to obliterate that light which
crosses every frontier.

Mankind is therefore only one organism, and unless we
realize this fact all that we do will be useless or, worse than
useless, will be pernicious for its healthy development.

Now this is the lesson that is learned by human beings, as
a result of all the movement that precedes the war and all
the movement that follows it. And at the present moment,
what we find in world affairs is a mixture of these three
ways of understanding world life, deeply blended, deeply
intertwined, not merely some of them in one nation and
some in the other, but all of them in all the nations, and
not merely all of them in all the nations but all of them
in all the individuals. All of us carry within us, whether we
realize it or not, a mixed international philosophy, a mixed
conception which contains, in our way of reacting toward

world affairs, the competitive, the coöperative, and the organic sense.

Now this is not necessarily an error or an obstacle to growth, or a mistake. In a human body there are elements which are organic. But there is a certain element of competition in the fight between the good and bad elements in the blood and in the cells; and there is probably also a certain element of coöperation.

In an organism such as that of world life or of national life, which is of course, though an organism, less strictly so than a living individual organism, it is natural that there should coexist organic elements with coöperative elements and with competitive elements. The healthiest situation for any one nation would be when its citizens, while realizing the organic character of the nation, maintained nevertheless within the nation certain activities under the ægis of coöperation, and even certain other activities under the ægis of competition. Nature is far too complex; nature is far too delicate, too incalculable, for it to be reduced to any one of the theoretical conceptions of any human mind. And therefore no undue depression or pessimism should be developed from the fact that at the present moment we are, all of us, under a kind of blended philosophy of life in world affairs which contains the organic, the competitive, and the coöperative element. The pessimism comes in, or at any rate the concern comes in when we observe that in certain powerful nations, nations that always were amongst the best of our Western civilization, the element of competition is reigning almost supreme, when we thought that, as a supreme element of life, we had driven it out of the picture at least one generation ago, if not longer ago. And the concern grows also—that is the second item of concern— when even within us these three conceptions of world life which, I repeat, there is no reason should not continue to coexist, are nevertheless somewhat uncoördinated and do not form for us a harmonious whole.

What is wanted, then, is first to see what we can do to drive out that element of international competition remaining in the world which is bound to end in war, and to see whether, within our own free and well-meaning part of the world, we cannot evolve a world philosophy, a philosophy of world affairs in which the three elements of competition, coördination, and organization, which coexist, cannot be brought into a more intelligent and coördinated synthesis. If we could achieve our second aim we should probably make great progress toward the first, but we cannot expect to be of much use in saving our more refractory brethren from their errors if our own philosophy of world affairs is not a little clearer.

# V

## A GENERAL VIEW

LET us now look back to the field of world forces we have been describing and try to see it in a general view, as a problem of coördination of these forces.

We are in the presence of a world organism. At the top, sixty sovereignties; in the body a narrower and narrower solidarity; very much as if we were beholding a monster with only one body and sixty heads. The life of such a monster cannot be very happy. Ours is not. Anarchy in the heads, because there are sixty of them to ponder what is going on, to judge it from sixty different points of view, to take sixty different decisions; but worst of all, anarchy even in the body, in that body of solidarity which we have been analyzing, because that solidarity is not yet organically coördinated, is itself a kind of anarchy.

There is first within this solidarity a total element or, to use a word in the fashion, a totalitarian element which tends toward world government. It is the solidarity which is exemplified in such institutions as the League of Nations, or the International Labor Office; a solidarity which implies that there is only one body and only one mankind, only one planet. If such were the only element in the solidarity that links together the peoples of the world, the fact that there are sixty heads would still remain as an element of considerable disturbance; yet the evolution toward the harmonizing of these sixty sovereignties into only one federation of solidarities would not be so difficult, but within that solidarity of the world there are other elements which complicate it. One is a number, rather intricate in its mutual relationships, of partial solidarities: such as the continental, the solidarity of alliances due to the fact that owing to certain traditions, friendships, certain connections are felt safer than other friendships and connections; spheres of influence, economic and financial control of one nation over another or, in less crude cases, economic and financial relations which deprive certain nations of completely free movement and make of them limbs in certain local bodies or congeries of nations and interests.

And further, there is an element of local partial solidarity which does not follow the national pattern, about which we have already said much in previous sessions—economic, financial, religious, political solidarities which do not follow the national pattern but pull this way and that, are to a certain extent international tegument and tissue; but because they do not adjust to the national pattern are in one sense good, in that they link together the nations, in another sense bad, in that they make it more difficult for all of these national organisms to coalesce into one.

So, in taking stock of the general situation we have to bear in mind not only the difficulty of the sixty heads, which are leading today the human nation, but also of the fact that the very solidarity from which we should expect our redemption is itself extraordinarily intricate, complicated, and full of internal forces which do not by any manner of means act always in a harmonious direction.

### RETARDING FORCES
*Sovereignty*

This situation presents elements of pessimism and elements of optimism. In the system of forces which we are considering, some are retarding forces in the evolution of

mankind toward its full consciousness as a world commonwealth.

Among the retarding forces, sovereignty is of course the
most important. We have already dealt with it at large. It
is not necessary to do more now than to mention it so that
it is established that we have not forgotten it. Evidently the
fact that every time we try to coördinate the efforts of the
sixty nations, that element of sovereignty rises before us
and rises in us, is living inside all of us as well as outside, is
one of the most important retarding forces in our evolution.

### Memories of the Last War

The second, so far as the moment of history in which we
happen to live is concerned, is the memories of the last
war. Memories which have remained living not only in the
consciousness of the peoples that took part in it—some of
them thinking and feeling still the humiliation of their
defeat; others realizing the vanity of their victory, and
others, again, trying to get free once and for all of the en-
tanglements which made them participate in the last war
and which did not result in the advance and progress and
glory for peace which they had expected at the time.

These war memories also act as a retarding force, un-
happily and unluckily in the actual efficiency and working
of the League of Nations, for they have been, as they could
not help but have been, incorporated in the Covenant, and
more than in the Covenant—in certain articles of the Treaty
which gave over to the League machinery a number of international duties arising out of the war, a fact which has
been undoubtedly one of the most important elements not
only in the lack of efficiency of the League but in the lack
of sympathy toward the League which in many of the

nations has been one of the factors for the retarding of its
evolution.

## Fear of the Next War

Then there is another retarding force in world affairs,
this time not emanating from the last war but from the
next war, the fears of the next war. These fears act in many
ways and all of course unfavorable, for fear is a bad counse-
lor for nations, as it is for human beings. First, it increases
the skepticism of nations about the possibility for the
League of Nations to keep the peace of the world, and it
creates therefore within every nation a current counter to
the current of mutual trust and confidence which is at the
basis of all League and, indeed, of all world-peace efforts.

Then it tends to develop in all nations what is nowadays called by an awkward word corresponding to the awkward thing it represents—*autarchy,* the tendency to make
the nation economically independent of any other nation
in case there is a war and the nation has to rely only on its
own sources of supply. That produces the economic nationalism from which the world is suffering and which in its
turn produces again an increase in mistrust. We are so
locked up in a vicious circle—fear of war leads to seeking
economic self-sufficiency; and this hunger for economic self-
sufficiency leads to fear of war and the preparations for a
possible war. Fear of war is, then, one of the most important
retarding forces in our evolution toward the world commonwealth.

It acts, moreover, in a third most unfavorable manner;
under its influence, the efforts of the civilized world are
diverted from the organization of the usual constructive
activities of mankind, to the organization of a war-avoiding
or a war-preventing or a war-punishing system. Now, if we

concentrate our minds on the avoidance of war we are concentrating our minds on war; while what is needed is to concentrate our minds, not even on peace but on the development of the usual humdrum activities which people pursue in peace; the fear of impending war has therefore prevented the normal and healthy development of our world institutions along the lines which they should have naturally followed.

## Mental Reservations

This retarding element is closely connected with another psychological feature of the present age, and of all ages, but acting today as an important factor in our evolution. Most of us are apt to keep mental reservations at the back of our minds in case what we believe does not come true. Even those nations, even those parties within those nations which believe in the necessity of world peace keep a mental reservation in case it does not work. This reservation may be general or special: a general reservation covering the whole philosophy of peace and constructive confidence: Is it a fact? Are we sure that mankind is going to agree to work together in peace? Or are those right who claim that man is incurably a beast and that he will always try to do his very worst for man? In short, is man a wolf or man? as the Latin poet said; or should we trust him to behave like a son of God? This problem is insoluble; only experience can tell. But evidently, if we are going to take the part of the wolf, we certainly are going to weigh the scales heavily on the side of pessimism, and it is up to us to fight on the side of the angels.

We may then transfer, or translate, to the language of world politics and the faith in peace one of the most beautiful utterances of de Sénancour about the existence of

God: "Let us so behave that if God does not exist it be an injustice."

## Fascism and Nazism

And then there is no question that at present we are in the presence of a specific historical difficulty in the process which interests all of us, namely that in the midst of Europe, in two of the nations which for centuries have been of the most brilliant and the most profound contributors to civilization, schools of political thought have turned up which deny all we believe. Fascism and Nazism consider with contempt any idea of pacifism, any belief in the possibility of world peace and of the coördination of the men and nations of the world along peaceful activities. There they are, in the midst of Europe, two powerful and intelligent nations, holding these views—at any rate officially; and how can we avoid observing the fact and realizing that it is having on our evolution a double negative effect, one in so far as those two powerful nations are not helping us, the other one in so far as their very existence and example and the prestige of their cultures is having a powerful effect on the public opinion of the others and making them shake in their convictions.

## Obsolete Habits

Another retarding force is to be found in the political habits which our contemporary nations have inherited from previous days and which are not so easily shaken. Our European nations, and perhaps I may be allowed to say those that are not European, have inherited habits of dealing in international affairs and in diplomacy not unlike those of gypsies selling horses, making subtle arrangements, sidewise arrangements, silent arrangements, arrangements leading to what is believed to be, rather naïvely, national profit and certainly incompatible with the spirit of open and frank diplomacy asserted in the Covenant.

Now it is impossible to say that these old habits have disappeared. They continue. They coexist with habits that directly contradict them, but we are all familiar with the capacity of human beings, whether individual or collective, for carrying on incompatible systems of behavior at the same time. Under this category I should also refer to the habit of carving the world into spheres of influence in which to spread the particular financial, economic, cultural power of this or that particular nation.

### Imperial Evolution

In close connection with this retarding effect, we must also admit that imperial evolution, if only by example, by the effect and stimulus of example, leads the nations that have recently come to fulfillment to follow the same path which nations that arrived at their full nationhood in previous moments in history have opened. The feelings thus created are a powerful retarding force in world affairs.

### Old Wine in New Bottles

All this leads yet to another habit which is also having a retarding effect, perhaps more important than at first sight might appear—the habit of pouring old wine into new bottles, of using the League of Nations and the Covenant for the aims of diplomacy and of military supremacy and of financial oligarchy which are not in consonance with the spirit of the Covenant; but the Covenant has been found often a convenient instrument for achieving such nationalistic aims. Anyone with direct experience at Geneva knows, for instance, that nationalism, far from being absent in Geneva, flourishes there in an extraordinary way. I would venture to say that it flourishes there especially, and this is not to be wondered at. Imagine the person of an individual who lives in an isolated position in spiritual and physical isolation such as, for instance, a shepherd might enjoy in a lonely valley or hill. He will probably be much less conscious of his personality, though more immersed in it, than any of us who live in the midst of other men. Similarly, the nation that stays at home is less conscious of its nationalism than the nation that goes to Geneva and mixes with the other nations. The first effect of the League of Nations has therefore been an extraordinary increase in nationalism because it has dramatized it; all correspondents who have gone to Geneva have known how to exploit this fact and how to dramatize it and put a whole nation behind every one of the men who went to speak before the forum of nations in Geneva.

This dramatization of the relations between nations has evidently had a stimulating effect on nationalism, and it is a typical example of the devious ways in which evolution can act, for though ultimately the League of Nations, or any form of world government built on it, is bound to reduce nationalism, the first effect of its existence has certainly been a profound stimulation of it. Indeed human psychology, whether individual or collective, is so unexpected that there has developed in Geneva a kind of nationalism of internationalism, and every nation takes a nationalistic pride in being the most non-nationalist or unnationalist or internationalist nation in the world.

### Isolationism

Yet another of the retarding elements that we find in our path is the tendency toward abstention or isolation in international affairs. This tendency is particularly strong in the United States. But it is existent, it is alive in every one of the nations of the world, including those that belong and are most active in League affairs. It is particularly strong in the three nations that have left the League—Japan, Germany, and Brazil—and in the nation which has left the League in spirit without leaving it in law—Italy.

### Weak Sovereignties

Finally, surprising as it may be, a retarding element in world affairs is sometimes due to lack of sovereignty on the part of certain nations or peoples. When a nation is so weak that it cannot "put up" enough sovereignty, this fact in itself creates a retarding element in our evolution, because it overemphasizes sovereignty in other nations or groups of nations. As Vinet admirably said, "In order to give yourself, you must own yourself." Before the free and complete service of nations is available for the federation of nations, those nations must exist fully as such.

### Accelerating Forces
### The Actual Existence of World Government
### A. As a Rudiment of Government

Let me now come to the other side of the picture and briefly describe what I consider to be the accelerating forces in the evolution of the world toward unity, consciousness, and government. The first of all is the fact that, thanks to the League of Nations, there exists already a rudiment of world government. Those superficial minds—when they are grown up we may call them superficial; when they are young we just merely call them hurried, or impatient—who condemn the League of Nations, who believe that, because it has failed once, twice, three times, or ten, and may still fail a hundred times, they should scrap it, do not realize how precious is the fact that that nucleus of world government is there, tangible, and we know what it is. We know the building, we know the men, we know the office, the telephone number, and the people who are going to answer the telephone when we call. These things appear to be trivial; they are really most important. Imagine what the world would be if all that did not exist, if that nucleus of human beings and of relations of law and of practices and of habits and periodic meetings had not already established some kind of gear which has caught the nations of the world and no longer lets them go. Even the vested interests; even the fact that there are four hundred people drawing salaries out of no nation but out of the federation of nations is a hopeful element, an accelerating element and the kind of anchor that keeps the idea of federation there so that it cannot be any more torn out of the set-up, and that is the first triumph which we owe to President Wilson, that idealistic though people think he was—and undoubtedly was— he held to his idea of creating the League, even in the unfavorable and deplorable conditions of the Treaty because it was better that the League should be born out of an unworthy mother than that it should not be born at all. And he was right. And along with it the fact that, thanks to the League of Nations, we have already evolved an international or world civil service, which may be better or worse, may sometimes be brighter than at others, may sometimes have a more international spirit than at other times but is there, exists there, and has already acquired the habits that make it a reliable instrument for the study of world affairs from the world point of view, even though this utility is at times veiled and at times hindered by the overpowering influence of the governments and executive instruments and bodies of the League of Nations.

So we have permanence, we have technique, we have method, we have tradition, we have all those virtues that at the center of a community create and irradiate the spirit of the community.

## B. As a Source of Community Spirit

A community spirit is being slowly created by the League of Nations, even apart from the inherent capacities of the Secretariat. From a cursory point of view, the League of Nations is nothing more or less than the nations of the League, and many of the problems that must puzzle people as to the incapacity or sterility of the League of Nations are due to that fact; we cannot create things *ex nihilo,* and we cannot expect the League to be any more than the nations that compose it. Cynically, one might say that you cannot expect the League to succeed any better than you could expect to make a fresh omelet out of twelve rotten eggs. Cynically, because though this is true, though it is the truth, it is not all the truth, and those who speak of the League as if it existed about, beyond, and above the members of the League of Nations are not altogether wrong; they are wrong if they believe that there is a spirit that hovers over all the members of the League, as soon as they get together.

## C. Moral Pride

This is yet another of the accelerating forces which have come into operation beyond the imagination of those who created the League. When the nations of the League are together, the spirit that they create is in advance of the most advanced of them; there is a kind of pressure, due to moral pride. Nationalism in Geneva has a tendency to take on the garb of international virtue. There is rivalry for being the most virtuous nation in the world which leads all these nations in Geneva, if not to behave as best they can, to speak as best they can about their behavior. You may say this is hypocrisy. You will be right. But I am not sure that I am as critical of hypocrisy as I was when I was young. Perhaps I have grown into a hypocrite; perhaps I have discovered the virtues of hypocrisy.

### D. Value of Hypocrisy

An illustrious Frenchman once said that hypocrisy is the homage which vice pays to virtue. We might just as well say that hypocrisy is the first station on the line that goes from vice to virtue. For we begin by behaving badly and not caring two pins about it; then we behave badly and just do not like to think about it; then we behave badly and do not like it; and then we behave badly and hide it; and it all ends in our behaving a little better. Hypocrisy is a mask, but it is not a mask made of cardboard; it is a mask made of flesh and sinews and, as it is in living communication with our soul through our body, our soul acts on it but it acts on our soul, and if we keep right on wearing a mask of saintliness for several years, we must end in saintliness. That is what is happening in the most unsaintly nations in the world.

There is a moral pressure in Geneva which was once exemplified by a confidence from the foreign secretary of a nation in the east of Europe, who said that when he left his country, his capital, several days' journey from Geneva, he started with a terrific speech directed, in his mind, against the particular nation that his own nation had in its mind's eye. And every mile that the train sped toward Geneva the speech became milder and milder, and when he arrived in Geneva he found, to his great surprise and the dismay of his countrymen, that his speech was quite amiable.

### E. Reason as the Only Plane of Union Among Strangers

Why is that? That is because human beings that belong to the same nation, the same herd, can agree on any plane they wish and generally agree on the easiest, which is the lowest—they agree on the plane of blood solidarity, and that is why a crowd composed of the members of the same nation tends to bear down and to run along animal passions. But people that belong to different nations cannot agree on that plane; there is little that is common among them on the animal plane and they can agree only on the higher plane of reason. So either they disagree and disperse —and their moral pride prevents them from doing that— or they agree on the plane of reason and therefore they have to make an effort upon themselves and rise to that plane.

Hence it is that delegates, members of different communities, still so uneducated about their need for solidarity, agree on a plane of reason in Geneva, and when they go back home fall back on the blood plane and forget all about the Geneva agreement. What force can strengthen and give permanence to the good effect of such gatherings?

### F. Organic Tension

Possibly the last of the accelerating factors that remain to be envisaged, namely, what we call the organic tension of the world. There is already in the world an organic unity, and this fact creates a tension toward unity whether we like it or not. That is the main force which is bringing together all the nations into an organic whole, and even the force that inspired the draftsmen of the League of Nations Covenant. Though this Covenant is based mostly on mere coöperation, certainly more on coöperation than an organic sense of humanity, it was this organic tension that was already acting on those men and made them write the document—the admirable document—which is the Covenant, the excellence of which can best be appreciated when one has had to deal with it constantly in the presence of immediate difficulties at the table of the League.

### The Actual Problem for Governments

Having thus examined the black and the white aspects of the world picture, let us now consider the problem as it appears to governments. Governments come in for a tremendous amount of criticism on the part of many writers on international affairs; governments and what they call diplomats. There are witty people who think that if all diplomats were put on a ship, and the ship was given permission to go all over the world and never touch on any land, international affairs would be automatically solved. It is just less witty than silly. It merely forgets the essential elements in international affairs.

To begin with, in this period of telegraphs and telephones, the diplomats are no longer anything but the mouthpieces of their governments. The ambassador of Philip II, near Queen Elizabeth, who heard from his royal master about every six months and feigned to hear only once a year, was quite happy to develop a semi-independent policy and probably did it much better than the bureaucratic King behind him. But today any ambassador anywhere, even across the seas, can be rung up by his government practically every day—and generally is—so let us dismiss such talk about diplomats. Though people may congregate in Geneva, they are the mouthpieces of the governments in the sixty capitals of the world. In reality, thanks to the telephone and the telegraph, today the governments meet in Geneva but remain at home simultaneously, and what is to be considered is not so much the position of the diplomats as the position of the governments.

Now the governments are in a very difficult position indeed; a position which is hardly appreciated by the critics who so easily shoot at them. There is a French poem by one of the poets of the late nineteenth century which describes a swan in the water, "between two infinites," one above and one below him. The governments are persons who are supposed to think between two inextricable sets of problems, at one end all this world landscape, which we have been trying to describe, of unbelievable complication, danger, responsibility; at the other end a public opinion of unbelievable complication, exigence, and ignorance; and between these two infinities of complication, these governments are supposed to act, and to act quickly, and no wonder that more often than not they fail. It is not that they are not well-meaning; most of them are. It is not that they are incapable; most of them are very capable; it is that they are dealing with questions of the utmost difficulty and with urgent matters of the utmost complication.

## Two Concrete Examples

A study of the theory and practice of international relations may well end with an illustration of actual governmental difficulties, taking two quite concrete examples, not as they actually occurred. We are not going to penetrate, nor can we, into the councils of the two nations we are going to consider; we do not know them, but we are going to try to interpret, to the best of our ability, what their position was, and thus to illustrate the tremendous difficulty which is nowadays, for any government, the carrying on of international affairs.

## Denmark in the Italo-Abyssinian Dispute

Let us consider successively the position of Denmark, a small power, and of Great Britain, a big power, in the question of sanctions which arose on the Abyssinian difficulty. We will first take Denmark, a typical small nation. What is her position in this world? Denmark is one of the most enlightened and orderly democracies that the world knows. It is world-conscious, desirous of realizing a world community as few nations are; it is peaceful to the point of being disarmed. It is the neighbor of Germany and therefore a nation that has often been bound to look very closely into the system of sanctions, so that when the treaty of guarantee was discussed at the beginning of the disarmament negotiations, a treaty which granted almost automatic application of sanctions on behalf of all nations in case of aggression, Denmark put in some reservations as to the possibility of applying sanctions in certain cases, for you will observe that if a small nation like Denmark just on the skin of that big nation Germany, with an economy which is very largely dependent on Germany as well as on England, is to apply sanctions, if only economic sanctions, Denmark is going to injure herself far more than she injures Germany; and that is one of the paradoxes of the system of sanctions. She is moreover, and rightly, preoccupied with the military situation in which she would be put if she were to apply military sanctions—a great danger for a small

country near Germany—and even with the military impli-
cations of economic sanctions to Germany which Germany
might consider as an unfriendly act and answer in a military
way.

Apart from Germany, her economy is strongly knit up
with that of Great Britain to such an extent that Denmark
cannot afford to disregard the public opinion of Great
Britain, for if this public opinion disagreed heartily with
Denmark on a very important point, a boycott of Danish
goods on the English market might be deadly to the Danish
economy. Her ideals, her cultures, her traditions, even her
policy link her up with the Scandinavian neighbors and
cousins, and finally she has her own political parties to
contend with, some of which favor a particular line of world
policy and a particular set of nations, others a different line
of policy and a different set of nations.

When the problem of sanctions arises in a concrete case
such as that of Italy, what is this government going to do?
Is it going to make its decision quickly, and is it an easy
decision to make? Can we throw bricks at them because they
take their time and hesitate? Are they vacillating and weak
because they lack decision, or are they merely thinking hard
as to what is the best course for them to take? Their world
consciousness says, "Let us go ahead; we must vindicate the
law. We cannot consent to what is happening. A world
crime is a crime against us." And their sense of immediate
responsibility makes them wonder whether they are not going to create a precedent on sanctions which is going to
bind them to the automatic application of sanctions against
Germany tomorrow, with mortal effects for their economy
and even perhaps for their very existence.

And then, what are the real intentions of England? Are
they going to be out in the open, leaving the most important

protagonist in the matter of sanctions behind, exposing themselves to the odiousness of the sanctions on the power and of its friends, without knowing exactly what England is going to do? And if they follow England, is that a digni-fied position to take for a nation that has her own opinions?

Now I am not suggesting what the Danish Government should have done; I am merely illustrating the tremendous difficulties that a well-meaning cabinet of ministers had to weigh, in one sense going one way, in another sense going another way, some people urging them to go ahead, other people urging prudence and slow work. Not all of the slow-ness in the workings of the governments of the League, and therefore of the League itself, is due to incapacity, to steril-ity, to stupidity; very often it is due to intelligence, to wisdom, to political sense.

### Great Britain in the Italo-Abyssinian Dispute

And now take Great Britain; today a highly world-conscious public opinion—unbelievably so for a big power, an opinion that is sincerely desirous of rapid progress toward the world community; yet with untold imperial responsibilities, direct imperial responsibilities because even for those who are not imperially minded, the British Empire is an organic growth—you cannot just cut it off or destroy it by dynamite, or suddenly change its constitu-tion. These things do not happen. The English have to observe and be faithful to their imperial responsibilities, therefore to their defense, therefore to the Suez Canal line, therefore to keeping all that system in a healthy condition for the imperial responsibilities which are the basis of all their political thinking—withal, an illogical and empirical people, capable of holding simultaneously several ideas that may not be quite compatible, some out of tradition,

others out of hope, some due to the skepticism of an old
people, others due to the ideals and generosity of a world-
minded people. And then a nation conscious of its greatness
and power, desirous to enforce the law of nations, and yet
to avoid provoking others to think that she is bullying,
particularly in a case in which it was difficult to see the
difference in actual fact between the vindication of the
League of Nations and the vindication of the British interest in Africa.

And then her dominions; what did they think? There
was a time when in this country everybody thought that
America should not join the League because England had
six votes in the Assembly. But anyone who observed events
knows that, if I may say so without lacking in respect, England is the dog wagged by its six tails. And when can Great
Britain move without knowing what the United States is
going to do? That is unthinkable. Now there is nothing
in Geneva more difficult than to know what the United
States is going to do. And then there was Hitler! We say
in Spain that there is no bullfight more difficult than when
two bulls are in the ring; and there are two bulls in the
European ring nowadays. And one cannot look at Rome
without a squint at Berlin.

If we take all this picture in, and apply it to the question
of sanctions in Abyssinia, we realize that the position of the
government of Great Britain was not easy. Did she lag behind? Everybody looked at Britain and said, "Well, let
us wait and see what Britain is going to do; we are not going to risk our friendship with Italy, we small people, when
Great Britain, who is the big power in the affair, does not
risk it, and we do not know but there may be an agreement
underneath—you never can tell with those Britons." Did
she come forward and get herself at the head of the troops

against Italy and for sanctions? Everybody said, "Great Britain is not wanting to punish Italy; it is because it suits her empire that she is doing it." So Great Britain had to move with the utmost caution. What was it all about? British Empire or the Covenant? And then was she going to put all her forces in the battle? Was she going to risk her navy, which is to the British Empire what the throat is to the human being, in a battle of new technique, never tried before in the narrow seas of the Mediterranean? And then were there no commitments whatever with Italy? And then her businessmen, were they very keen to upset the Italian system and plunge Italy into Communism?

The slowness and vacillation of the British Empire and its government were therefore not altogether due to weakness or to an incapacity to make up their mind. They were mostly due to the fact that world affairs today have become so hopelessly complicated that even the most powerful governments do not find it easy to make up their minds.

### CONCLUSION

It seems now evident that international affairs, as handled by national governments, are not merely as difficult as, but infinitely more difficult than, national affairs. And the proof of it is that of late, since the War, there is everywhere a strong tendency for statesmen to prefer the foreign department of the state to any other department; they seek the most difficult ministry because they feel instinctively that it is there that the publicity is concentrated and there that they can make the best career. Foreign affairs have become the most difficult affairs that any government has today to transact.

Now it will be impossible for any government to make a success of foreign affairs until it realizes that, to a great extent, perhaps to a complete extent, there are no longer, really speaking, *foreign* affairs; there are only *world* affairs. Foreign affairs have ceased to be foreign because they have a national background of great complexity and force; they are no longer foreign, they are world affairs, and all the ministers of foreign affairs should be rechristened *ministers of world affairs,* if only from the educational point of view, to drive into public opinion this view, that it is now the world that matters and not merely those foreigners who do not belong.

Moreover, it is not going to be possible for ministers of world affairs to solve the problems raised by these affairs unless and until they combine on a permanent system for carrying them on. That is to say, unless the ministers of world affairs or similarly powerful statesmen constitute permanent councils of world government—this League or a reformed league or a different league; personally, I think this League—but let us not be dogmatic about that—a world council for world affairs. And that, again, is going to be insufficient unless behind the world council for world affairs we create a powerful élite of world citizens, endowed with the necessary world patriotism to give to those world statesmen their inspiration and their guidance.